Crossing to Avalon

Crossing to Avalon

A WOMAN'S MIDLIFE PILGRIMAGE

Jean Shinoda Bolen, M.D.

HarperSanFrancisco
A Division of HarperCollins*Publishers*

Permissions begin on page 303.

FIRST EDITION

Library of Congress Cataloging-in-Publication Data
Bolen, Jean Shinoda.
Crossing to Avalon : a woman's midlife pilgrimage / Jean
Shinoda Bolen. — 1st ed.
p. cm.
Includes bibliographical references and index.
ISBN 0–06–250112–7 (alk. paper)
ISBN 0–06–250112–7 (pbk.)
ISBN 0–06–251109–2 (intl. pbk.)
1. Bolen, Jean Shinoda. 2. Women psychoanalysts—United
States—Biography. 3. Women—Religious life. 4. Midlife
crisis—Religious aspects. 5. Grail. 6. Goddess religion.
7. Pilgrims and pilgrimages—Europe. 8. Europe—
Description and travel. I. Title.
BF109.B64A3 1994 150.19'54'092—dc20
[B] 90–55174 CIP

94 95 96 97 98 ❖ RRD(H) 10 9 8 7 6 5 4 3 2 1

Contents

Storytelling, you know, has a real function. The process of the storytelling is itself a healing process, partly because you have someone there who is taking the time to tell you a story that has great meaning to them. They're taking the time to do this because your life could use some help, but they don't want to come over and just give advice. They want to give it to you in a form that becomes inseparable from your whole self. That's what stories do. Stories differ from advice in that, once you get them, they become a fabric of your whole soul. That is why they heal you.

ALICE WALKER,
in an interview about her work in
Common Boundary, 1990

Preface

We usually imagine the Grail as a chalice, most often as the chalice filled with wine that Jesus held aloft at the Last Supper, saying to his disciples as he did so, "This is my blood. . . ." His words and motions became ritualized in the Christian communion.

When we consider that as a rounded container a chalice is a feminine symbol, the idea of a vessel filled with blood becomes an image-metaphor for a woman's womb, and the Grail then takes on the possibility of another meaning—that of a numinous or mysterious feminine symbol, something transformative and healing, with a sacred or divine dimension of the feminine. In the most famous of the Grail Legends, there is a wounded king whose kingdom is a wasteland. His wound can only be healed by the Grail, and until his wound is healed, his kingdom remains devastated. Substituting patriarchy for "kingdom," this myth has considerable relevance today. Deforestation, famine, and armed hostilities, bad as they are, pale in comparison to the ultimate fate of an earth facing potential nuclear or ecological disasters that could turn the entire earth into a wasteland.

The legend of the Grail also has considerable psychological relevance. If we are living in a spiritual wasteland of depression, despair, fears, anger, meaninglessness, emptiness, or addictions, an understanding of the legend can teach us something about what ails us and what can heal us.

On the eve of a new millennium, something momentous is happening. We can see "the Goddess" re-emerging everywhere—as concern for and the resacralization of the planet, as a new appreciation for the feminine aspect of divinity, as an awareness of the sacredness and wisdom of the body. Images of goddesses are coming forth in dreams, in art, and in poetry. Once again, the Earth is seen as a living organism, as Gaia, the Greek goddess of the Earth.

I see the emergence of goddess consciousness as a return of the Grail into the world, a return that is for now liminal; that is, on the threshold, still between the worlds, emerging out of the mist, perceived by many and yet not fully present in the culture. The Goddess becomes known in embodied sacred moments. In order for her to emerge into the culture and change it, enough individuals must become aware of those deep and sacred moments in which a woman and the Goddess are one in the same—when Earth and Goddess and Mother and Woman partake of divinity.

The need for return of the Grail and the Goddess is, as I have experienced its meaning, a personal and planetary story about wounds and healing, about hope and wholeness.

ONE

Invitation: Pilgrimage

I opened the bulky envelope that had come in the day's mail and found an invitation that would change my life. A total stranger was inviting me on a pilgrimage. She intended that I might "experience my spiritual sources" and so was proposing a pilgrimage to sacred sites in Europe. I recognized the names of some of the places she suggested I visit—Chartres Cathedral in France; Glastonbury, England; and

Iona, an island off the coast of northern Scotland. And she had timed the trip so that I could meet the Dalai Lama, who would be in the Netherlands when I arrived. The packet contained the letter of invitation, dated February 6, 1986, from Mrs. Elinore Detiger of the Tiger Trust, the Netherlands; a check; and a beautiful handmade gold pendant in the shape of a *vesica piscis*. I would later find that this was the same design as on the wellhead of the Chalice Well at Glastonbury, the well in which the Grail was once supposedly hidden.

Glastonbury, England, was a place that had been alive in my imagination for years, ever since I had had a dream through which I made a connection with this site. Here exist the ruins of what was once the greatest Christian abbey in Britain, which was reputed to be the site of the first humble church to be consecrated to Mary, the mother of Jesus. Glastonbury was also the fictional location where one could cross through the mists to Avalon, the realm of the Goddess.

This amazing gift of pilgrimage actually had its origins in Glastonbury, where through a series of coincidental events, my book *Goddesses in Everywoman* had reached Mrs. Detiger. A woman from Glastonbury had visited San Francisco several months before and had been given a copy of *Goddesses in Everywoman* by a friend who also knew me. She had then taken it back to Glastonbury and was in the midst of reading it when Mrs. Detiger paid her a visit, discovered the book, and decided to bring its author to Europe. Originally, she had thought that she was supposed to bring me to Europe to speak about the women's movement, and then something—call it her intuition—made her extend this invitation to go on a pilgrimage instead.

The invitation came when I was in a muddled, painful, and perplexing time of my life. I was forty-nine years old and was trying to get my bearings; in the previous year I had separated from my husband after nineteen years of marriage and now was in a period of uncertainty. It was a very difficult period of transition and disillusion, and yet it had an unexpected richness. I was finding refuge in solitude, and in spite of the lack of external support for what I was doing, I had an inner conviction that I was following a soul path, even if I could not see where it was taking me. Like the return of sensation after circulation has been cut off or numbed by cold, I was also painfully and uncomfortably experiencing feelings of anxiety that I had held in my body and had not been aware of when the marriage was ending. My intellectual understanding had served as a defense; I had gone into my head and had become cut off from my feelings. This was the situation when Mrs. Detiger's invitation to go on pilgrimage arrived. It was not just the contents but the synchronicity of the date of the letter itself that made an impression on me that this was an out-of-the-ordinary invitation: on this day one year before, matters had come to a head in a confrontation that led to a separation and eventually to divorce. I wondered what ending or beginning this letter might portend.

My letter in response began:

There is so much synchronicity (which you could not know of) in the timing of your letter, the plans you are proposing, the places and people you have in mind for me to meet, that I am awed. I have tingles up my spine. Somehow this trip feels like a continuation of an unfolding midlife path, an initiatory rite perhaps, and certainly an introduction to something I only have vague intimations about.

I went on to say:

Your letter arrived during a period that gnostically feels like a gateway, a mythic moment of time and place (like the approach to Mount Analogue, if you are familiar with that strange book). This is a time of liminality for me, of passage from one part of my life to another, when I am venturing psychologically out beyond 'my known world,' heeding a call to live my life more authentically even as it puts me in conflict and uncertainty.

The book I referred to was *Mount Analogue* by René Daumal, a small book that I had read when I was in medical school. Like all stories that touch some deep truth, it had remained with me, much as a significant recorded dream might that is thought about, reread, and more fully understood only later. In the story a group of companions set out on a quest to locate the ultimate symbolic mountain, Mount Analogue, that united Earth and Heaven. The mountain is located on an island hidden by a curvature of space that deflects the light from the stars and also the lines of force in the earth's magnetic field, and thus acts "like an invisible, intangible rampart; *everything takes place around it as if Mount Analogue did not exist.*"

In Daumal's words: "To find a way of reaching the island, one must assume the possibility and even the *necessity* of reaching it. . . . At a *certain moment* and in a *certain place certain persons* (those who know how and wish to do so) can enter."

The companions find the island and begin the ascent of the mountain. In midsentence in the fifth chapter, midquest, the book ends. Midquest is also where the first known version of the legend of Perceval and the Grail, written by Chrétien de Troyes, ends. Daumal died before he could complete his book. From some notes he left behind we know that the title of his last chapter was to be "And You, What Do You Seek?" This is the same question I pose to my lecture audiences when I ask, "Are you on a Grail Quest?"

Without defining what I mean, I often find that the question evokes an inner affirmative answer in many people, who respond, as one does to the Grail, to the personal meaning it has for them, even though what the Grail *is* remains unclear and mysterious.

Might each of us who answers yes be on a quest for something that is not only missing from our own lives but from our culture as well? To have an inkling, an intuition, a clue as to what we seek may bring the Grail closer. By sharing the stories of our personal journeys and telling of our encounters and what we learn of the Grail, we each might contribute to the possibility of returning that missing Grail to the world. This is my premise.

Beginnings

Significant mythic journeys begin at a juncture when exceptional circumstances initiate a heroic response. For Bilbo Baggins in J.R.R. Tolkien's *The Hobbit,* answering a knock on the door to admit Gandalf the Wizard began an adventure that would take him into a dragon's lair. For Psyche in the myth of Eros and Psyche, the journey began only after she tried to drown herself and was thrown back on the bank by the river. Pan, the god of the countryside, happened to be nearby to advise Psyche to cease grieving and seek Eros, which led her to Aphrodite and the challenge of completing four initially impossible tasks. Perceval's quest began when he saw five knights in shining armor and was so dazzled by them that he took them for angels (his mother had told him that angels are the most beautiful beings apart from God), and on finding they were knights, set out to become one. And Ayla, in *The Clan of the Cave Bear* and *Valley of Horses,* twice ventured out alone, first as a five-year-old child after she had been orphaned by an earthquake, and then as a woman who set out to find others like herself.

In *The Hero with a Thousand Faces,* Joseph Campbell writes that the hero's journey begins with the Call to Adventure: "The call rings up the curtain, always, on a mystery of transfiguration—a rite, or moment, of spiritual passage, which, when complete, amounts to a dying and a birth. The familiar life horizon has been outgrown; the old concepts, ideals, and emotional patterns no longer fit; the time for the passing of a threshold is at hand."

Whether by choice (usually the hero's position) or by necessity (usually the heroine's situation), a person heeds the call, and the stuff one is made of—the soul—emerges as challenges and losses are met on the journey.

Passing Through the Gateway

In fairy tales, legends, and science fiction, the main character often arrives at a "gateway" that is both a special time and a special place. Here and now, she or he must choose whether to step through and go beyond the known world: Only once in a hundred years does the impenetrable briar hedge that surrounds the sleeping maiden part to allow the prince to pass through; a protagonist in a science-fiction fantasy can enter the stargate or portal to another dimension only if he or she gets there at a precise time; Mount Analogue can be approached only from the east, at sunset, at the time of the solstice; and it was only at Glastonbury in King Arthur's time that the barge could be summoned to take one through the mist to the Isle of Avalon.

The idea of passing through a gateway or doorway is reflected in the psychological word *liminality,* which is derived from the Latin word *limen,* meaning "threshold."

Jungian analyst and author Murray Stein describes midlife transitions as periods of liminality, which I think aptly describes those times in our lives when we are in an "in-between" zone, a state in which we are neither who we used to be, nor who we are becoming. It's like standing in a doorway, or being in a passageway, or even in a long dark tunnel, between two phases of our lives.

At such times, we are often thin-skinned and vulnerable, which accompanies being psychologically receptive and open to new growth. Most of us can remember being so in adolescence, another time of major transition. At such times, we resemble a snake, the ancient symbol of transformation, which must shed its old skin in order to grow and while molting and growing a new skin is vulnerable, irritable, and, for a time, temporarily blind.

During times of passage, we also may find ourselves in a liminal psychological state, which is what the poet T. S. Eliot is describing when he writes of "the point of intersection of the timeless / with time," that place of poetic sensibility where glimpses of the eternal and ordinary perception overlap. Here the invisible spiritual world and visible reality come together; here intuitive possibility is on the threshold of tangible manifestation.

During liminal times, we often become aware of *synchronicity*, a word coined by C. G. Jung to describe coincidences between our inner subjective world and outer events. Synchronicities such as the uncanny and timely appearance of a significant person or opportunity are often choice bringers. Will we respond? And if we do, will it usher in a new phase of our lives?

Think about the timing with which a major teacher or opportunity or love presented itself in your own life. At some other time, you might not have responded to this same person or opportunity at all. In periods of stability, we are too involved or too busy with what is at hand to respond to a call to adventure. We are simply not available. There are also periods of depletion when we cannot respond to anything new, however attractive the invitation might be. This is a psychological analog to the physiology of nerve conduction. A stimulus will not evoke a response in a nerve while it is already "excited" and involved in conduction, nor in the period immediately afterward when the neurochemical involved is depleted.

Only in periods of availability will a person respond to a call to adventure or love, and thus to the lessons it will inevitably bring. The Eastern saying "When the pupil is ready, the teacher will come" describes this synchronistic connection between inner readiness and outer event.

The invitation to go on pilgrimage came during such a time. I was receptive and open to what might come next. My teenage children now spent half the time with their father and would be with him during the period while I was away. Without hesitation, I made the choice to step through this gateway and became a pilgrim.

TWO

Meeting: The Dalai Lama

As I set off for Europe, awed that my first event was to be a private audience with the Dalai Lama, I wondered whether I would feel a "guru whammy," which is my expression for the impact that people describe experiencing on meeting their guru. For I was on my way to meet a living legend and a great spiritual leader. What could I anticipate? What would he be like? I felt like Perceval setting off on a Grail Quest, and well imagined that on this trip I might prove to be the innocent fool who, on being shown the equivalents of the marvels in the Grail Castle, would not know what questions to ask.

Just before I left for Europe, my local bookstore happened to display the biography *Great Ocean: The Dalai Lama.* I picked it up (I call this kind of experience "book synchronicity"—it often happens that the right book turns up when I need it) and I found out that the Dalai Lama's full name is Tenzin Gyatso, his Holiness the Fourteenth Dalai Lama of Tibet. He is considered a Bodhisattva, a great soul who has achieved enlightenment in a previous life and has voluntarily reincarnated on earth to help others. Prior to the 1959 invasion of Tibet by the Communist Chinese, he was the absolute spiritual and temporal head of his country, and he now headed a government-in-exile in Dharmsala, India. I also was interested to find that he is only a year older than I and that he is considered an incarnation or manifestation (the word he prefers) of Chenrezi, the divinity of Compassion, the deity or awareness-being of the heart.

A Private Audience

The day arrived on which I was to meet him, and "a private audience" turned out to be an informal gathering in a Dutch castle. There were a dozen or so of us awaiting him. The Dalai Lama came into the room wearing a maroon robe over a yellow garment, followed by other similarly dressed monks. He shook hands with and greeted each of us. When it was my turn to meet him, he gazed directly into my eyes, smiled, shook my hand, said hello, and made chuckling, chortling sounds, very much like the noises made by a happy baby, which I had never heard a grown man make before.

He seated himself among us. He was proficient in English and open to any question. Here was the opportunity to ask him *anything*. What would you ask the Dalai Lama, especially if you recalled Perceval, who, on seeing the Grail, failed to ask a question, thus causing the Grail to disappear, the king not to heal, and years to go by before he could see it again?

I did have a question that was more than a bit esoteric. It was, however, the only genuine question I had for him. On doing research for *Gods in Everyman*, I had wondered if there was a connection between Tibet and the Greek god Apollo, whose temple housed the Delphic Oracle. I wondered whether the Tibetans were the "Hyperboreans" that the Greeks referred to, whose name either meant "Beyond the North Wind" or "Beyond or Above the Mountains." It was said that Apollo visited with the Hyperboreans for three months every year. The historians of the time had considered this a real place.

I also remembered from reading his biography by Roger Hicks and Ngakpa Chogyam that there seemed to be a link between Tibet and the Hopi Indians. When the Dalai Lama had visited the United States in 1979, he had met a group of Hopi elders, who pointed out that his arrival fulfilled an ancient prophecy of the Hopi nation. "According to Hopi traditions, the world's axis passes through both their land and Tibet. At the end of a thousand years of Hopi religious practice, a great spiritual leader would arrive from the East: He would be the Sun Clan Brother, and his name would be linked with salt water. 'Dalai' means 'Great Ocean,' and 'Gyatso' means ocean." As it happens, there is an equivalent Tibetan prophecy: "When the iron bird flies and the horse runs upon rails, the Dharma (teachings) will travel west to the land of the Red Man. . . . There are many other similarities between Hopi culture and Tibetan, including some very curious ones: The Hopi word for 'moon' is the same as the Tibetan word for 'sun' and vice versa."

Since Tibet, Delphi, and the Hopi nation all were or are spiritual centers that valued prophecy and ritual, it seemed right to me that they might have been in communication. For I envision these places in my mind's eye as centers of light, linked by strands of light that span the globe and connect sacred places. Geographical distance surely wouldn't have been a barrier for people who could have communicated telepathically or through out-of-body experience.

And so, hoping he would comment, I asked whether Tibetans were the Hyperboreans, and the connection between Tibet and Delphi and the Hopi.

The Dalai Lama listened intently to my question, said hmmmmm, and then was silent and smiled, leaving me to my own intuition and imagination.

Musing upon This Meeting

The impact of my visit with the Dalai Lama would come later. Words were not important; his presence was. I had come to this audience with him thinking that I could not remain silent like Perceval, so I asked the only question I had on my mind. As I continued on this pilgrimage, however, it became clear to me that the Grail questions—those Perceval failed to ask—were the important ones: "What ails thee?" and "Whom does the Grail serve?" Furthermore, they were questions I did not need to ask the Dalai Lama but myself, questions that each of us needs to ask if we are to heal what ails us. If we ask the right questions, the answers can come. If we seek the Grail, we may find it, for, as I keep learning, the mysterious healing Grail is hidden in people, in places, and in experiences.

As I thought about the significance of meeting the Dalai Lama, I was reminded again of the saying "When the pupil is ready, the teacher will come." In this case, when I was receptive to what he symbolized, the insight came. In his joyfulness and unselfconscious chortling, he had the spontaneity of a happy, trusting child and he was a compassionate and wise teacher. In the previous decade, I had lost the spontaneity, wonder, and vulnerability that I once had as I had become increasingly responsible for more people. I needed to be in touch with the child within *my*self who could truly feel my own feelings and act upon them. I realized that "what ailed me" was directly related to what could heal me. And when I could be as unselfconscious as a trusting child, intuitively moved to respond in the moment, I would find that I also was in touch with the wise woman who knew what was true in myself, as the Dalai Lama so beautifully exemplifies.

Each time I discover some personal truth such as this, I realize that it was there all along. It is, in other words, available wisdom, there to be rediscovered by each of us if only we can see it. The link between the truth-speaking, trusting child and wisdom, for instance, is archetypal. When we read that Jesus said that we must become like children to enter the Kingdom of God, which is at hand, his words make immediate sense; to perceive anything divine or numinous requires the capacity for awe and wonder that is a natural ability of the innocent child, who still sees the world as magical.

The magical child archetype appears in the dreams of people who are getting in touch with meaning or creativity in their lives and sense that they might have a personal destiny to fulfill. In their dreams they perhaps give birth to a special child or meet a child who is in some way exceptional: The dream child might be a beautiful newborn baby the size of a two-year-old or an infant who looks at the dreamer and talks; it might be that a voice in the dream announces the baby and his or her name. On awakening the dreamer will recall the dream with pleasure and often with puzzlement: who is this child?

Characteristically this is a dream that arises in conjunction with a new connection with the archetype of the Self, the archetype through which we derive a sense of meaning and affiliation with something greater than our small selves. The dream appears with the possibility of new or renewed life. The soul is awakening.

The symbolic figure who heralds a new beginning, or holds the promise of transformation, may appear in any guise in a dream, not just as a child. When we have such a dream, notes Joseph Campbell in *The Hero with a Thousand Faces,* "there is an atmosphere of irresistible fascination about the figure that appears suddenly as guide, marking a new period, a new age, in the biography. That which has to be faced, and is somehow profoundly familiar to the unconscious—though unknown, surprising, and even frightening to the conscious personality—makes itself known."

Sometimes someone actually appears in our waking lives upon whom we project a part of the dream of who we could become. Such a person can be as symbolic as a dream figure and imbued with the same quality—the promise of new life and meaning. They attract us with a promise—a potential to heal us—which we either correctly intuit or miscast upon them. Had I projected onto the Dalai Lama the possibility that he could heal me, make me whole, and evoke the divinity in me, I would have been moved as people are when they meet their guru. I would have "fallen in love" with him. But that didn't happen.

It is not just gurus who receive these projections, but also psychotherapists, or anyone who becomes larger than life and intensely attractive in this same way; when there is a call to the soul, we do fall in love with the person—who may be of the same or opposite sex—upon whom we project these yearnings to be seen and loved as divine and beautiful beings.

While the person who captures such projections and thus captivates us may have qualities that drew the projection, others not similarly enchanted do not see what we are seeing; they are not "in love" as we are. When we project soul upon another person, we are drawn out of our mundane lives by the numinosity of such an attraction; it is a spiritual, erotic, and mysterious call, which stirs us inwardly and is likely to disrupt our lives. Such attractions may seem destructive, to resemble the attraction of moths drawn to light, because what often follows is a phase of deconstruction of structure and disassembling of priorities, the metaphoric death of some phase of our lives. This may also lead to disillusionment. Projections cannot be sustained. What happens when he or she turns out not to be as magical and wonderful or spiritual as we had imagined? We may then be plunged into a period of confusion or darkness that is about the soul.

Out of an often-unrecognized need to lead a spiritually meaningful and emotionally authentic life, we project soul upon someone, something, or some belief that then draws us. If the new perspective or the attraction then disrupts our lives and what drew us away from our former stability loses the magic, a dark night of the soul results. Like the Knights of the Round Table who saw the Grail at Camelot and set out to find the Grail in the wilderness, attraction and loss can be an initiatory experience that takes us into unexplored and undeveloped psychological and spiritual terrain. Many adults in the midst of what others depreciate as a midlife crisis are on a spiritual quest. I certainly considered this to be so for me.

When I received the letter inviting me to go on pilgrimage, my marriage was dissolving and I was on my own; I was no longer on a well-trod and defined path. Involvement in a grassroots women's spirituality organization had awakened a deep wish to lead a more authentic life; I had not thought that where this would take me would be out of my marriage, but it had. The book I had written as a psychological text on the goddess archetypes in women had become a best-seller. In evoking images of Greek goddesses, I had invited the return of a Goddess consciousness in women; it was as if I had opened a gateway into a parallel world where divinity had a feminine face, where the body and the earth were sacred, and where ordinary events became enhanced by spontaneous rituals, and I was among the first to go through that gateway. The thought of pilgrimage and the timing of it sent tingles up my spine because it felt like a continuation and affirmation of a quest I had unknowingly begun. It felt like a call to my soul and a Grail Quest.

This mysterious quest for the Grail underlies many midlife attractions, be they toward a soul mate or soul work. When this is so, there is an aura of promise around this new person or task.

Once we understand this we can appreciate elements in the Grail legend that may help us to discern the compelling power of the call—and the potential of setting out on the Quest and becoming lost in the Forest and not even knowing what it is, this Grail that we seek.

THREE

Quickening: Chartres Cathedral

*Let us spare a thought for those who century after
century, took the pilgrim's staff, whether they were
pagan or Christian, and set out by roads which were
hardly tracks, across rivers that were hardly fordable,
through forests where the wolf hunted in packs,
through marshes of shifting mud in which poisonous
water snakes lurked; subjected to rain, wind storms,
sharp hail, sunstruck or frozen, at night the only
shelter a flap of their tunic pulled over the head; all
this having left home and family not knowing if they
would see them again, in order to reach at least once
in their lives a place where divinity dwelt.*

LOUIS CHARPENTIER, *The Mysteries of Chartres Cathedral*

Of all the sacred sites that Mrs. Detiger had planned to have me visit, Chartres Cathedral was the one that I most looked forward to. Chartres had exerted a pull on me ever since I took art history at Pomona College. In the darkened classroom I had seen the magnificent stained glass windows, flying buttresses, and soaring arches projected on the screen; in the midst of a survey course acquainting us with art from the time of ancient Greece to the present, Chartres seemed to hold something special for me as a place and as an expression of an unprecedented flowering of architecture and spirit in the twelfth century. I remembered that historians were puzzled as to how and why so many Gothic cathedrals were built in a relatively short period; their construction required a concerted outpouring of effort, talent, energy, and financial resources beyond what seemed possible. Of them all, Chartres Cathedral stood out in my imagination. Now, finally, I was a modern pilgrim on my way there.

In marked contrast to the hardships of pilgrims in the days of old, I only had to take a short flight from Amsterdam to Paris and then an automobile ride from Paris to Chartres. When I arrived in France, it was spring and Paris was beautiful. I was to be taken to Chartres by a guide whom I was to meet at the American University. Such was not to be the case however; the guide had had an accident and an American woman who loved the cathedral offered to drive. But once there, I would be on my own.

The next morning she picked me up in front of my elegant hotel. We left Paris and were shortly on a highway that made its way through fields and small villages in a gently rolling landscape. Nothing stood out on the horizon until we made a turn on a rise in the highway and there, unexpectedly close by and silhouetted dramatically above the pastoral countryside, was Chartres Cathedral. I caught my breath, as one instinctively does in the presence of great beauty or mystery.

Next thing I knew we were there. I walked into the gracefully proportioned cathedral and found a group of visitors gathered around an English-speaking guide. I gravitated toward them, listened for a while, and found that this was not what I wanted to be doing. I knew that there was a labyrinth on the floor somewhere and I went in search of it. I found it in the nave, occupying a circular area almost the width of the church. There were rows of folding wooden chairs over it, so it was hardly noticeable. I decided to walk the labyrinth, which required that I move each chair, one by one.

This was not the kind of maze one gets lost in. There were no blind endings but instead a path that would take me over every bit of the figure to the center, which, with its circle and six lobes, looked like a stylized flower with petals. The path to the center was its stem. Encyclopedist

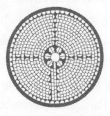

Barbara G. Walker comments that this design is associated with Aphrodite, Greek Goddess of Love and Beauty.

Later I learned that labyrinths were originally associated with caves and were usually situated at the entrance. In the coolness and dimmed light of the thick-walled cathedral, with the great vault overhead, one can imagine being in an enormous high-ceilinged ritual cave, with its stalagmite and stalactite columns and mysterious labyrinth in the floor. This symbol of the Earth and the Goddess can be found not just here at Chartres but in at least twenty other cathedrals throughout Europe, including Poitiers, Toulouse, Reims, Amiens, Caen, Cologne, and Ravenna. I discovered that Chartres Cathedral, like many other Christian cathedrals devoted to the Virgin Mary, was built on a pilgrimage site that was, prior to Christianity, sacred to the Goddess.

Mary was held in particular veneration at Chartres. In the very word *venerate*, the goddess Venus (Aphrodite's Latin name) is hidden. Émile Male, an authority on Chartres, writes that "it was the great centre of worship for the Virgin; the cathedral appeared to be her dwelling place on earth. At Chartres, when the hymn 'O Gloriosa' was sung in her honor, all the verbs were given in the present tense, to demonstrate her presence."

Henry Adams, whose book *Mont-Saint-Michel and Chartres* is a classic, concluded that "Chartres represents not the Trinity, but the identity of the Mother and Son." Mary's cathedral was built where, long before Christianity and even before the Greeks and their deities, the Goddess was once worshiped. Typically, the Great Goddess had a myriad of names. Here at Chartres, she continues to be worshiped in her aspects of virgin and mother, only instead of being called Isis, Tara, Demeter, or Artemis, her name is Mary.

Just as places where the Goddess was worshiped became sites for Christian churches, so too were her symbols taken over. Before becoming Mary's symbol, for instance, the open red rose was associated with Aphrodite and represented mature sexuality. At Chartres, which is dedicated to the Virgin Mary, roses abound. Light streams through three enormous and beautiful stained glass rose windows, and a symbolic rose is at the center of the labyrinth. The path of the labyrinth is exactly 666 feet long. Six hundred sixty-six, according to Barbara Walker, was Aphrodite's sacred number. In Christian theology it became a demonic one.

In the western aisle of the south transept, another mystery was built into the cathedral. Here, according to Charpentier, who writes of the esoteric qualities of Chartres Cathedral, is "a rectangular flagstone, set aslant to the others, whose whiteness is noticeable in the prevailing grey of the paving. It is conspicuous for a shining, lightly gilded metal tenon" (the insertion portion of a joint). Every year on the summer solstice (approximately June 21), a ray of light comes through a clear space in the stained glass window named for Saint Apollinaire and strikes this particular stone exactly at midday. Like the presence of a labyrinth, the timing here hints strongly of an Earth-oriented Goddess tradition embodied in this Christian cathedral.

After I walked the cluttered labyrinth with some difficulty and very little meditative concentration, I wandered through the great church looking at all there was to see. Thus far I was strictly a sightseer, not a pilgrim. Just before leaving on this journey, I had heard that a Druidic well and a black madonna had been found at Chartres. As it turns out, Goddess sites almost invariably have holy wells or springs. I decided to inquire about the possibility of seeing the crypt under the church and found that the shopkeeper at the small gift shop adjoining the cathedral led small groups through the crypt.

When it was time for the tour, a small group gathered, and she locked up her shop and took us to a side door of the cathedral, which she unlocked, and we descended until we were under the church. She spoke in French, which I don't understand, but I read an English description of what she was showing us and heard partial translations of what she was saying from some of the others. Now her friendly and bored shopkeeper expression was gone. Here in the crypt, her passion showed. It was clear that we were with a person who loved this place. Her general demeanor changed. Something about her look made me think she could be a short, solid, medieval friar, with a rope around the waist. And I thought, who knows, perhaps she was.

In the crypt, there is indeed a well, now covered with a locked lid, which is as deep as the taller spire of the cathedral is high. It is an ancient Celtic well about thirty-three meters deep that was once in a grotto. In this low-ceilinged, cool, cavelike, dimly lit chamber under the church, it was easy to imagine a grotto. Long before the Christian era, pilgrims had come to this site and were reputed to have found next to the well a statue of a dark goddess, which was later called a black madonna. She may have been a representation of Isis, the Egyptian mother goddess. Isis was a black goddess whose dismembered son Osiris was resurrected as Horus. Isis was probably the original black madonna, whose worship spread through the Greco-Roman world. Now, in the cathedral above, there is also a black madonna. She is a traditional Roman Catholic figure of Mary wearing a crown, but her features are black.

Once the tour to the crypt was over, there was time for me to return again to the cathedral. Only this time, something in me had changed. I was no longer the tourist; I had become the pilgrim. The descent to the grotto had affected me greatly, and almost as if in response, as I walked into the cathedral this second time, the organist began to play and the magnificent sound seemed to vibrate through the stones and through me.

I found that I was not taking things in primarily with my eyes and mind anymore. I was instead feeling my way, perceiving the energies in the cathedral with my body, responding to the place kinesthetically. For the first time in my life, I felt myself acting like a tuning fork or a dowsing rod. I was aware of something that was neither pressure nor vibration nor warmth, yet seemed to have qualities of all three, centered in the middle of my chest between my breasts and radiating in all directions. As I walked through the cathedral, I found that what I began to think of as "the tuning-fork effect" was greater in one place than others. When I stood at the intersection between the nave and the transepts in front of a cordoned-off altar area, the intensity was the greatest.

Standing there, I felt like holding my arms outstretched, and I had a sudden insight: If I were the same size as the church and were laid out, my arms the length of the transepts, the labyrinth was where my uterus would be. It occupied the "womb" of the church.

Quickening

When new life stirs within the womb, and a mother has the sensation of her baby moving within her for the first time, it's called "quickening." The same word is associated with pilgrims, who go to sacred places to "quicken" the divinity within themselves, to experience spiritual awakening or receive a blessing or become healed. The seeker embarks on a journey with a receptive soul and hopes to find divinity there. And, as I began to appreciate from my tuning-fork response to Chartres, pilgrimage to a sacred place is an in-the-body spiritual experience—as were my pregnancies.

It is believed that the divine spirit is incarnate at sacred places, both in the sense that the Deity is present there and in that these are places where the divinity penetrates matter, impregnating or quickening the divine in the pilgrim. In Europe, places of Christian pilgrimage are nearly always sites that had been sacred to the Great Goddess before the advent of Christianity.

Charpentier notes that Chartres Cathedral was built on the site that was once the Druids' sanctuary of sanctuaries, on a mound or elevation where there was a sacred wood and a well that was called "The Well of the Strong." Here, carved in the hollowed-out trunk of a pear tree, once existed a statue of a dark woman or a goddess with an infant on her knees, believed to have been made by Druids before the birth of Christ.

The power of the place is in its location. Here ancients came to receive "the Gift of the Earth; something Earth gives like a Mother." Here human spiritual faculties were awakened by what the Gauls called the *Wouivre*, the telluric (magnetic or cosmic) currents that "snake" through the ground and are represented symbolically by serpents. Dolmens or megaliths (large stones) were placed where these currents are particularly strong.

Drawing on esoteric and historical sources, Charpentier says that a particularly strong current comes to a head under the hill on which Chartres Cathedral is built and accounts for its unusual northeast orientation (cathedrals are usually oriented toward the east). He says that a megalithic stone or dolmen may lie buried in the mound and that it is because of the sacredness of the ground upon which the cathedral stands that among all the cathedrals in France, Chartres is the only one that has no bodies buried in it.

Learning of the *Wouivre* brought other images to my mind: of the famous bas-relief of an unidentified Greek goddess—thought to be Demeter, the Goddess of Grain and mother of the maiden Persephone—arising out of the earth with a snake, wheat, and flowers in each hand; of a Minoan statue of a goddess or priestess, arms outstretched, holding a snake in each hand; of statues of Athena with snakes on her shield or in the hem of her garment, symbolic remnants of her pre-Olympian origins. Might the Great Goddess, who was in her various manifestations Earth Goddess/Mother Earth, be the provider of sacred energy (the snakes) as well as flowers and wheat? This would explain the images.

In Eastern religions, sacred energy, called *kundalini,* is also symbolized by a snake that lies asleep at the base of the spine (as if in recognition of the significance of this location, in Western anatomy we call the protective shield-shaped bone that covers the end of the spinal cord the *sacrum*), until it is awakened ("quickened") and rises up through the chakras through spiritual practices. In Eastern physiology, the human body (like the Earth) is seen to have meridians running through it, with acupuncture points at junctions. These points can be stimulated to reduce pain, heal the body, and restore balance and harmony.

On this pilgrimage I first heard of telluric currents and first experienced for myself this energy that is present at places where humans have worshiped for thousands of years, and it occurred to me that sacred places are the "acupuncture points" of the Earth. But I continue to experience the tuning-fork phenomenon, and as a result I tune into the environment wherever I am. I simply quiet my mind and try to feel the response of my body. I tune into an instinctual awareness of the quality of the energy that permeates a place, a sensory intuition that extends to people, animals, trees, and even rocks. In Ireland, for example, I "met" standing stones—each one like an ancient, patient, and wise presence. On a Greek island I came across a grove of old trees in a ravine that had such a malevolent quality, I could not bear staying there.

Mrs. Detiger has the idea that when we visit sacred sites, we are not only affected *by* them, we also are awakening their dormant energies. Maybe so. Maybe the Australian aborigine whose sacred task it is to sing his or her particular piece of the songline that keeps the soul of the earth alive is not superstitious and ignorant but is doing exactly that. Maybe we can be attuned to Nature; maybe communing with Nature is a sacred dialogue, upon which our spiritual development as a species depends. It was only through my own pilgrimage that I became aware of these possibilities and began to develop a conscious relationship to the Earth as Mother—a living being made up of matter and energy, as are we, with our visible bodies and invisible psyches.

FOUR

The Grail Legend:
The Spiritual Journey

Both a pilgrimage and a Grail Quest are outer journeys and inner experiences. Both pilgrim and questing knight leave behind their usual lives and go in search of something that they are missing, not necessarily knowing what that is. Such is especially the case with the Grail. As I set out on this pilgrimage with the Grail story in mind, I was aware that the story itself is elusive;

there are many versions, contradictions, and interpretations, and I was about to add my own.

If *we are spiritual beings on a human path rather than human beings who may be on a spiritual path,* which I intuitively believe to be so, then life is not only a journey but a pilgrimage or quest as well. When we experience sacred moments it often is not so much a matter of outer geography but of finding soulful places within ourselves. The labyrinth as an image and the Grail legend as a story are then both metaphors that can help us become aware of the spiritual dimensions of our personal lives.

I began to think that the labyrinth in the nave at Chartres can serve as a symbolic map or metaphor for the pilgrimage. Once we enter it, ordinary time and distance are immaterial, we are in the midst of a ritual and a journey where transformation is possible; we do not know how far away or close we are to the center where meaning can be found until we are there; the way back is not obvious and we have no way of knowing as we emerge how or when we will take the experience back into the world until we do. There are no blind ends in a labyrinth, the path often doubles back on itself, the direction toward which we are facing is continually changing, and if we do not turn back or give up we will reach the center to find the rose, the Goddess, the Grail, a symbol representing the sacred feminine. To return to ordinary life, we must again travel the labyrinth to get out, which is also a complex journey for it involves integrating the experience into consciousness, which is what changes us.

34

The Grail legend, with its many different stories and versions, expresses an essential human mystery and holds an implicit promise within it: the potential for wholeness, healing, and meaning. It is one of the central myths of the second Christian millennium, its protagonist a hero on a spiritual quest. The story vividly expresses the psychological journey toward wholeness that C. G. Jung called "individuation," which he considered the task of the second half of life.

Grail Legends, Dreams, Storytelling

The many variations on the Grail legend that we're familiar with were written in the twelfth and thirteenth centuries but they undoubtedly tap a much earlier oral tradition. The legends express the spirit of that particular time, a period of cultural flowering during which the great Gothic cathedrals were built, the concept of romantic love was first introduced, veneration of the Virgin Mary first became important, and the Crusades expanded the European medieval consciousness by contact with other more developed cultures. Though they reflect their particular time, the stories of the Grail are also timeless and archetypal, relevant now as then.

As a Jungian analyst, I have been listening to people's dreams for almost thirty years and have found that reading about the Grail is like listening to dreams. If you can recall a dream of your own that contained something that puzzled you, it may illustrate this point. When I listen to people tell me their dreams or when I think about my own, there are symbols in them—many of them unfamiliar—that the dreamer does not consciously understand. But symbols are part of human history and mythology; they have a collective meaning across time and geography. In everyone's personal dream life, there is evidence of a collective source that we tap into when we dream.

Artists and writers whose work touches us deeply instinctively access collective symbols. They "dream" for us; they bring images and stories from their own depths that could be our own. If we are conscious, we recognize ourselves in them. Otherwise we only know that we are moved. Seen from this perspective, artists or authors are our contemporary versions of shamen who have visions for their tribes. They tap into a deeper stratum and express it. And that stratum—the collective unconscious—draws upon more than the culture of the time or the experience of that particular individual, although both color what comes from this timeless, transpersonal source. This understanding helps explain the emergence and the contents of the Grail stories.

The familiar Grail legends were written by men, the most famous versions by Chrétien de Troyes (about 1180), Robert de Barron (about 1190), and Wolfram von Eschenbach (1207). De Troyes did not finish his story of Perceval's quest, but there are three other notable continuations. The legends came out of a masculine, patriarchal, and Christian time and culture and yet they are also filled with pagan influences, which is probably why the Church never embraced them. Within these variations on the Grail legend are symbols and references that are found in Celtic and Greek mythology, in Arabic poetry and Islamic imagery, in Tibetan and Egyptian ideas, and much more.

Who does the telling, shapes the story. Recall the classic Japanese movie *Rashomon* and the principle it demonstrates. A man is murdered and a woman is raped, and four people tell what happened. Each person's version is "true," yet each version tells a different story. It *matters* who does the telling. And as *The Mists of Avalon* brought home, though the events around which the story hinges are similar, the story of King Arthur and the Knights of the Round Table is a different tale when told from the perspective of the women.

In one version of the Grail legend, the Grail appears at Camelot at Pentecost, then disappears, inspiring the Knights of the Round Table to seek it. Many suffer, most do not return, and only the pure knight Galahad finds it. In *The Mists of Avalon,* the Grail that appears at Camelot is the cup of the Goddess, the cauldron of Cerridwin, and it is Arthur's half-sister Morgaine through whom the Goddess acts.

> Morgaine . . . lifted the cup between her hands, seeing it glow like a great sparkling jewel, a ruby, a living, beating heart pulsing between her hands. . . . She moved on, or the cup itself moved, drawing her with it. . . . She heard a sound as of many wings rushing before her, and she smelled a sweetness. . . . The chalice, some said later, was invisible; others said that it shone like a great star which

37

blinded every eye that looked on it. . . . Every person in
that hall found his plate filled with such things as he liked
best to eat. . . .

For the time, Morgaine feels the power of the Goddess
flooding her body and soul and filling her. She carries the
cup, and speaks as the Goddess: "I am all things—Virgin
and Mother and she who gives life and death. Ignore me at
your peril, ye who call on other Names . . . know that I am
One." And then the cup and the dish and the spear, the
Holy Regalia of the Goddess, disappear, taken by magic to
Avalon so that they will never be profaned by priests and
men who deny Her, and the knights scatter to the four
winds in search of the Grail.

It was this contemporary version of the appearance of
the Grail at Camelot that made me rethink the Grail stories as I knew them. Within me and within my own spiritual experience I had approached the Grail stories as they
were told by men—through the relationship of the male
characters to the mysterious, healing Grail. But when I
thought about the maiden who is the Grail carrier and the
Grail itself as feminine symbols, I recalled Grail experiences that I myself have had—experiences that were in the
body and of the body, sacramental moments that came to
me through being female and through the physical presence of women.

In the Grail legends, spirit, heart, and mind are the
three paths represented by the three knights who find the
Grail. Left out is the possibility of experiencing the Grail

through the body. That the sacred can be experienced through the body is everywhere denied by patriarchal religions. For the body to be considered holy once again, the Goddess (the feminine aspect of the Deity) must return, for it is only through a Goddess consciousness that matter can be perceived as having a sacred dimension.

Basic Themes in the Grail Legend

While there are different versions of the Grail legend, the basic story can be summarized as follows:

The Grail is a mysterious and profound object—it may be a vessel, a shallow dish, a stone, or a jewel—that is worth giving up the whole of one's life to find. It is in a hidden castle where the Fisher King lives. The king has a wound that will not heal, and his kingdom is a wasteland. He will be healed and his kingdom restored only if a knight can find the castle and, on seeing the Grail and the wounded king, asks a certain question, usually either "Whom does the Grail serve?" or "What ails thee?" If he fails to ask, the castle will vanish and the knight will have to set out once more upon the search. If he again finds the Grail Castle and asks the proper question, the king will be restored to health and the wasteland will turn green.

The Grail is most often imagined as a sacred vessel: the chalice used by Jesus at the Last Supper or, in another version, the one that held some of the blood that flowed from the wound in his side while he was on the cross. It was reportedly brought from the Holy Land by Joseph of Arimathea—who reputedly founded Britain's first church at Glastonbury—and then was lost. The image of a sacred vessel existed in pre-Christian Celtic and Druidic myths as the Cauldron of the Goddess, through which rebirth, inspiration, and plenty would come.

In the several versions, only three of the many knights who set out from Camelot on the Grail Quest actually see the Grail: Galahad, Perceval (Parzifal), and Bors. Galahad, the pure knight, finds the Grail and leaves the earth in a blaze of ecstasy; Perceval, the innocent fool, returns to the Grail Castle and becomes the new King and Guardian of the Grail; Bors, the ordinary man, returns to Camelot to tell the story.

In *The Grail Quest for the Eternal,* John Matthews comments that the three knights "represent three ways of approaching the mystery." For Galahad is reserved the way of the Spirit, of direct communion with the godhead; for Perceval the way of dedication, of the Heart, which entails a long, hard road toward self-realization; and for Bors, who watches the events but stands a little apart from them, the way of contemplation, of the Mind.

In my own *The Tao of Psychology* I wrote about the Grail. At the time I wrote that book I shared the same mystical Christian spiritual perspective that underlies the Grail legend itself and added a psychological interpretation that would help men and women who are successful but are feeling cut off from sources of inner meaning.

People seek psychiatric help for symptoms of depression and anxiety and the more serious related mental illnesses. Symptoms often clear and people function well as a result of psychotherapy, but I have noted over and over again that my patients also need a sense that their lives have meaning. I'd like to excerpt a long passage from *The Tao of Psychology* because I think it illuminates what this search for meaning is all about.

> There is a desolated country, a wasteland, where cattle do not reproduce, crops won't grow, knights are killed, children are orphaned, maidens weep, and there is mourning everywhere. The country's problems are related to the wounded Fisher King, who suffers continuously because his wound will not heal.
>
> The Grail is in his castle, but the king cannot touch or be healed by it until, as prophesied, an innocent young man comes to the court and asks the question, "Whom does the Grail serve?" The Grail was the legendary communion cup used by Jesus at the Last Supper and is a symbol of Christ or the Self (Christ and Self both describe something beyond human or ego, something that is divine, spiritual, reconciling, and gives meaning).
>
> If the ruler of the country, the ego, could be touched by the Grail and experience the spirituality of the Self or inner Christ, it would have the power to heal him. Synchronistically, when his wound was healed the country would recover. Joy and growth would return. The wound may symbolize the situation of ego being cut off from the Self, where the separation is a wound that never heals and

causes continuous pain in the form of persistent, chronic anxiety and depression.

The Fisher King's wound is the psychological problem of modern times. In a competitive, materialistic society, where cynicism toward spiritual values exists, and neither scientific nor psychological thinking gives any importance to the realm of the spirit, individuals feel isolated and insignificant. Seeking sexual intimacy to cure isolation or seeking assertiveness as a solution to feeling insignificant does not heal the wound. When the ego is cut off from experiencing the Self—or, put differently, when an individual lacks the inner sense of being connected to God or being part of the Tao—then a wound exists that the person experiences as gnawing, pervasive, persisting insecurity.

All kinds of defensive maneuvers, from smoking to amassing power, are unsatisfying efforts to feel better. The narcissism of modern times seems fueled by the feeling of being deprived and unnourished emotionally or spiritually, which is part of the same wound. A person thus wounded seeks novelty, excitement, power, or prestige to compensate for a lack of joy or inner peace. Chronic anger and depression seem to hide just below the surface of the persona, or face presented to the world. Again, this is a consequence of the wound, of the ego being cut off from the Self. This wound defeats the capacity to both give and receive love. Emotionally, scarcity rather than abundance prevails, and thus generosity, compassion, giving hope and helping all are constricted, and joy and growth are stifled.

To restore life to the wasteland, the Fisher King's wound must be healed. This can be equated with the ruling psychological principle of the psyche—that which the ego uses to determine value and make choices. For many individuals, and certainly for our culture as a whole, rationalism or scientific thinking is the ruling principle. In the Grail legend, it is cut off from the spiritual communion vessel, through which healing and return of vitality would flow. The wound that will not heal is a result of the severing of a connection crucial to well-being. The King cut off from the Grail is the rationalist cut off from spirituality, thinking separated from intuitive feeling, the "Type A" heart attack–prone, linear personality cut off from everything that is nonrational and gives meaning.

The King cannot touch or be healed by the Grail until an innocent young man—sometimes described as an innocent young "fool"—enters the scene. From the standpoint of the "ruling principle," which here is rational thinking, the wound will stay continuously open and unhealed until a new element enters the psychological situation. It may be that only the young, naive, innocent element within the psyche—which from the perspective of worldly thinking would be considered the fool—can experience the wonder and awe of the Grail, a Christ symbol, and can ask questions about meaning, which then can lead to a restoration of a connection between the ego and the Self. Then the internal landscape which has been a wasteland or dry desert, may bloom or be green again, as emotional and spiritual feeling, the irrational elements in touch with the symbolic layer of the unconscious, are brought into the personality.

My understanding of the Grail legend to this point had come from two sources: from my work as a psychiatrist and from a mystical experience that I had as I turned eighteen.

"Thy Will, Not Mine, Be Done"

Between graduating from high school and beginning college, I went to Forest Home, a Christian summer camp in southern California. It was up in the mountains, where I always felt closer to God. The expansiveness and beauty of the starry heavens at night put me in touch with a deep sense of awe and an awareness of being one with the Universe. Though I had gone to a variety of Protestant churches and had been baptized at twelve as a Presbyterian, my religious attitudes had been mostly a matter of accepting what I had been taught and being familiar with the form.

At this period in my life, I was feeling very good about myself. I had earned academic honors, won school elections, done very well in speaking and debating contests, represented my high school at a variety of events, and been popular with friends, all of which I felt I deserved. I planned eventually to go to law school, which I expected would be an easy path for me. It also would fulfill a dream that my businessman father had once had.

While this was before the "born again" movement, and the camp was sponsored by the largest Presbyterian church in the Los Angeles area, it had an evangelical slant and booked a number of charismatic speakers to come and address us throughout the summer. Listening to one of them, I suddenly felt ashamed of my pride and humbled; I realized that everything that I had accomplished was due to unearned gifts such as health, intelligence, talents, opportunities, and good parents. I had not done anything to deserve what I had been given.

In this state of humility, I went out for a walk. It was night and safe to walk through the wooded camp. Eventually, I went into an empty prayer chapel, lit only by a few candles, and prayed. It was there that this undeserving, prideful, humbled eighteen-year-old had a profound mystical experience of God, the loving, forgiving father, a moment of grace that changed me forever. In that chapel in prayer, I realized that I could never repay God for what I had been given but that I could express my gratitude by helping others who were less fortunate. In this state of grace, I prayed, "Thy will, not mine, be done" and in the profound silence that followed, I became convinced that I was directed to become a doctor.

In my college years, the conviction was sorely tested. Though I excelled in the liberal arts, which I loved, I did not have much aptitude, let alone love, for the premedical math and science courses. At midterm, I even got a warning notice of a D in invertebrate zoology, which I would have to bring up. Math and chemistry tests were trials, passed as much on luck that had me plug the right numbers into the appropriate equations, as on understanding. I even cried the night before a couple of chemistry examinations because the work was so hard.

At the same time, in every liberal arts course that I took, I could get a fairly easy A. My rational self started wondering about this path I was on; might I have mistaken the message? In my junior year, I made a bargain with my rational self: I would continue with premed but also do what I enjoyed in college. I would apply to medical school, and if I were not accepted, which was a distinct possibility, I would accept that I had made a mistake about what God wanted me to do.

Application time came and I was accepted at the University of California School of Medicine in San Francisco. It would be another five years, however, before I ambivalently and serendipitously began a psychiatric residency (thinking a year of psychiatry would be useful for whatever else I ended up specializing in) and discovered that this was work that I was meant to do—in the sense that it felt so right. I found that I had a gift for psychiatry, that my ability to genuinely care for my patients, to have an intuitive understanding of them and a fascination with the complexity of the psyche, served me and them well. A decade had passed since I had made my commitment to God to become a doctor, and it was simply the strength of the conviction that had sustained me until then. My lack of aptitude for math and basic sciences and the difficulties of premed and medical school were behind me; I had trusted and stubbornly persevered in doing what I thought I was supposed to do, and unexpectedly it was deeply satisfying. About this time, I came across a Sister Corita painting that said, "To Believe in God is to Believe that the Rules will be fair and there will be Wonderful Surprises."

The mystical experience of God that I had at eighteen was followed by a continuing sense of access to God through prayer. Only one other time did I experience the vivid and ineffable presence of God and the accompanying sense of being a recipient of grace in a Christian context, and that occurred in the midst of my marriage ceremony in an Episcopalian cathedral. It is the experience I drew from when I wrote about the archetype of marriage in *Goddesses in Everywoman.*

I was brought up as a middle-of-the-road Protestant. No mystery or magic accompanied our religious rituals. The communion sacrament was a commemoration that used Welch's grape juice. Thus it was both unexpected and deeply moving for me to find that my marriage ceremony in San Francisco's Grace Cathedral was an awesome inner experience. I felt I was participating in a powerful ritual that invoked the sacred. I had a sense of experiencing something beyond ordinary reality, something numinous—which is a characteristic of an archetypal experience. As I recited my vows, I felt as if I were participating in holy rites.

There are certain experiences that are simply ineffable. I experienced God as spirit, as an infusion of grace from above that was sacramental—it made the moment sacred. At the beginning of the path I would take into medicine I felt God's presence in a chapel and then again in a cathedral in the ceremony that began my marriage.

If these were my only numinous experiences of divinity, I would not be reexamining the Grail legend or adding the

Body (to the Spirit, the Heart, and the Mind) as a means through which the Grail is experienced. But I did experience divinity through my body, which I believe has to do with being a woman: a woman's body is the vessel through which the Goddess comes.

In traditional tellings of the Grail legend, there is silence about the woman who carries the Grail. She does not seek it, nor has she been separated from it. Her access, her experience of the Grail, is through her body. To discover the Grail story from her perspective is to enter the realm of the Goddess and women's mysteries—where Grail, Goddess, and Woman come together.

FIVE

Women's Mysteries and the Grail

Before introducing the sub-
ject of women's mysteries, we must resurrect the original
meaning of the word *mystery*. In most libraries, under the
heading "Mysteries," we find books about solving mur-
ders. In a spiritual context, however, a mystery is a religious truth that one can know only by revelation. It comes
from the Greek word *mystes*, which for at least two thousand
years prior to Christianity was associated with Eleusis, the

sacred precinct of the mother goddess Demeter and her daughter Persephone. The initiate, or *mystes*, had a profound transformative experience that he or she (for both men and women participated) was to keep secret. And the secret was maintained well into the Christian era (the rites were practiced until A.D. 396).

We all know that people cannot be depended upon to keep secrets, yet this one was never told, which points to the probability that it was a secret that could not be revealed through words. The mystery must have been the experience itself, an ineffable revelation that changed the participant into an initiate who, as we are told, no longer feared death.

What we do know is that the myth of Demeter and Persephone celebrates the reunion of the mother goddess with her daughter, who had been abducted into the underworld by Hades. We can surmise that, like Christianity, which is a father-son mystery religion, the mother-daughter Eleusinian Mysteries were concerned with death and return—as resurrection, rebirth, or reunion—and that the initiate in some way now could share the fate of the deity who overcame the realm of death.

The two mysteries are also similar in worshiping a Divinity with three aspects: Father, Son, and Holy Ghost comprise the Christian masculine godhead, while the Goddess was worshiped in her three aspects as Maiden, Mother, and Crone. At Eleusis, it may very well be that the Crone was also similar to the Holy Ghost in being a spirit. For according to the "Homeric Hymn to Demeter" that tells the story of Persephone's abduction, Hecate, the archetypal crone and wisewoman, Goddess of the Crossroads, *preceded and followed* Persephone from the time she emerged from the underworld—an impossible feat, unless Hecate was a spirit.

Initiation

To be initiated into a mystery psychologically is to have a mystical experience that changes you. You no longer are who you were before. You have undergone something that sets you apart from those who have not had the experience. Often an initiation involves an element of isolation, of facing fear or undergoing an ordeal. But perhaps just as often, the initiatory experience comes as a gift of grace, when mystery and profound beauty come together in a numinous moment of which we are a part. The new initiate feels archetypally twice-born: into life at birth, and now through a mystery, into a new state of being or new consciousness.

You might think it odd that I am *writing* about something that can only be known through personal experience. But what if women have been venturing unknowingly into sacred territory *and been without words* for the experience? Then what was felt deeply and never articulated, shared, or put into a context fades from conscious awareness. Without words or names for an experience, memory is hampered: it's a bit like not knowing how to access information that is stored in a computer, only much more complex because what is unconscious in us still affects our bodies, relationships, and dreams. Furthermore, only when we have words that fit what we know deeply is it possible to contemplate the meaning of an experience. We use words to remember and recollect as well. For example, when I've spoken about the "tuning-fork" sensation that I felt in the center of my chest at Chartres Cathedral, I have found that it has opened gates of memory and meaning for others.

From my previous writing about archetypes I also know that for readers, having words and images for what they have only known subjectively is like seeing themselves in a mirror for the first time. There is the possibility of reflection, and with it, the memory of events and feelings. And when there was a sacred dimension to that now-recollected experience, which is true of women's mysteries, a woman may recall that what she did not have words for had to do with the divinity within her, or the Goddess that is expressed through her, and the power or awe that she unaccountably felt in touch with in the moment. When such events now fall into place, a deep aha! results.

Even if this was not how it was for you, or if you have not had any such initiatory experiences, or if you are a man, reading women's mysteries can still ring true or feel right intuitively, because we are in the realm of archetypal experience and share a collective unconscious. However, because women's mysteries are *of* the *body*, there will still be a difference between what a woman might know with her mind—through her imagination or what she has been told—and the physical experience itself.

Musing about this led me to think about the difference between the abstract idea of childbirth, which I learned via lectures and textbooks in obstetrics, and the direct experience of being a woman in labor myself. As a medical student and intern, I observed contractions, timed them, checked on how the cervix was thinning out and dilating in preparation for the birth, and eventually delivered about a hundred babies myself—none of which did much to prepare me for the actual experience of giving birth.

Pregnancy as an Initiation

For me, pregnancy was an initiatory experience that changed my body, shifted my consciousness, taught me surrender, and was the beginning of the dawning awareness of the physical, psychological, and spiritual demands and gifts that would come through being a mother. Much later, I would come to see that pregnancy and childbirth are also experiences akin to living a myth, which occurs whenever we are in an archetypal experience.

Like puberty, pregnancy was something that was as much happening *to* me as *in* me. My body was changing physically and taking energy to do it. Especially in the first three months, I tired easily and slept more than usual. Then the shape of my body changed, and with it, my center of gravity shifted. As a result, I became physically unbalanced, fell, and injured my ankle. I felt a new kind of vulnerability, emotional as well as physical.

Something also happened to my psyche that I thought of at the time as a "biological introversion." With my Jungian orientation, *introvert* and *extravert* were familiar terms, and I knew what ordinary introversion was. This was different. I was definitely introverted but not in my head: I wasn't introspective or contemplative. Thoughts and images were not important. Instead, I felt as if the center of consciousness had shifted downward from my head and now vaguely existed somewhere in or above my growing uterus. The sense of "I" was now located in my body, and this "I" was contented to be still, like a rock on a riverbank in the sun as the river went by. I continued to work during most of the pregnancy, however, and was aware that it took effort to shift from this state of just being to being in my office, where I had to use my mind and heart to concentrate, think, intuit, and relate to others.

The inward pull of pregnancy seems to me similar to what happens in people who are dying, especially toward the end, when it is only a matter of time before the demise of the body takes one into the unknown, often feared, next phase. As either due date approaches, one's circle of interest narrows, and the problems and happenings in the outside world become unimportant.

Death of the old form and new life or birth are fundamental to initiations. In pregnancy, this happens on many levels, as a woman becomes heavy with child. She may have had an agile, energetic, and strong body, or a soft, sensual one. Typically, her figure was that of the maiden, and the attractiveness of her face was important. With pregnancy, as her psyche shifts and her maiden body disappears from physical sight, she changes archetypally, to herself and to others. Symbolically, the maiden dies in order for the pregnant mother to come forth.

Once she is obviously pregnant, a woman resembles the earliest sculptured images of the Goddess. She is an embodiment of the famous pregnant "Venuses," of which the Venus of Willendorf is the most well known. Made between twenty-five thousand and twenty thousand years ago, these goddess figures have heavy, pregnant bodies, no personal facial features, and legs that taper so that the figure could be put directly into soil. According to archaeologist Marija Gimbutas, "Pre-industrial agricultural rites show a very definite mystical connection between the fertility of the soil and the creative force of woman." That connection is emerging into the culture again. A mystical awareness, having to do with being in a woman's body and being part of Gaia as the living Earth, is revealing itself to women. (The intellectual understanding that we are as much a part of Gaia as the rivers or trees, which was formulated by James Lovelock as the "Gaia hypothesis," is an *of the mind* perception. I am speaking here of women's mysteries, which are *of the body*.)

When I first felt movement in my uterus and knew it truly was my baby, it brought a smile of wonder to my face. This was firsthand, in-the-body knowledge, verifying that there really was a baby growing inside of me. While it was a wonder to me that this was happening, being pregnant is commonplace and quickening just part of it. The patriarchy does not have rituals to celebrate such wonders. But suppose men got pregnant; I imagine that the ability to bear children would then be proof of the innate superiority of their gender, and a pregnancy would announce the beginning of a major rite of passage for an individual man that would be celebrated. Or if just one man miraculously became pregnant, this particular pregnancy and delivery would be treated as equivalent to taking the first steps on the moon.

This fantasy arises out of my understanding that patriarchy devalues whatever it is that women do naturally and instinctively. Behind this is the male God and the idea that men are created in the image of God. But for thousands of years prior to the Bible and to Zeus and the Olympians, humans worshiped the Goddess. So when I start to speculate about how pregnancy might be experienced by women if we valued what women do, I think back to my own experience of quickening in pregnancy. And I remember how it felt to have my body respond to the energy at a sacred site for the first time, and I recall that pilgrimages were undertaken to "quicken the divinity." Through these strands of recollection, I know intuitively that if the Goddess had not been obliterated from consciousness and culture, quickening would be valued as a profound religious experience. A pregnant woman would know that she shares in the essence of the Goddess as creator, who brought forth all life from her own body. Sensing her own divinity would occur simultaneously with feeling life stir within her own womb. At that moment, she could know and say, "The Mother Goddess and I are one."

My two children were born in the early 1970s, when the Protestant Trinity of Father, Son, and Holy Ghost was all I knew, before I had any inkling of the spiritual dimension of the feminine. And yet even then, when I felt life moving in me, I was aware, if only dimly, that there was something here about being a holy vessel. I had no words for it. Because my first successful pregnancy had been preceded by three miscarriages, I did not take it for granted.

While her circumstances make a considerable difference in how a woman feels about being pregnant, if Demeter, the mother archetype, is strongly present in her psyche and if her body and spirit have not been desecrated by physical or emotional abuse, then these words of the rosary directed to the Virgin Mary might well fit her experience: "Blessed am I among women, and blessed is the fruit of my womb." These words are close to voicing the mystical awareness that can arise in women in that moment of revelation when they know that they and the Goddess are one. Pregnancy is then the barge that takes a woman through the mists to Avalon and the realm of the Goddess.

Labor and Delivery

My husband and I had taken natural childbirth classes, seen a film, and read some books in preparation for what was to come. As the due date approached, I awaited the onset of labor as if setting off on an expedition or the first day of medical school. While I had never done this particular feat before, it evoked my can-do competitive spirit, and I intended to do it well. I had, after all, won grades and honors, delivered babies, and made it through medical school, an internship at Los Angeles County Hospital, and a psychiatric residency. At thirty-three, I was not a youngster. In the back of my mind, I did have some anxieties, but I kept them pretty well tucked away: Would the baby be normal? was my greatest concern. I considered the possibility that there would be complications. These were matters beyond my control. Many women also feel deeply fearful of what women know collectively—that terrible pain and death in childbirth are possible. These thoughts did not seem to cross my mind. In Greek times women would pray to the virgin goddess Artemis for mercy, either for a quick delivery of the baby or a quick death.

Contractions began in the early evening, growing stronger and more regular as the hours wore on. The first hours of labor were not bad, and it was easy to breathe the way I had been taught in childbirth class. It was a piece of cake really, which was reassuring. Thus, when it was time to leave for the hospital, it felt like an adventure to set out with my prepacked bag, cross the Golden Gate Bridge to French Hospital, and from there be taken to the labor and delivery area. My obstetrician was part of a group practice that had been the first in San Francisco to allow fathers to be present in the labor and delivery rooms. Thus I was not going through this by myself. I was in a supportive situation with my husband and professionals I trusted, and in a hospital setting that was familiar.

However, this turned out not to be familiar territory at all. Like the Sumerian goddess Innana who voluntarily decided to visit her sister goddess in the underworld and found that she had to go through a series of gates, at each one stripped of something that represented her identity and power in the upper world, so did I move. The first gate was the hospital admission process, where every patient surrenders her valuables and identification. At the next gate, she surrenders her clothes and is given a loosely tied gown to wear, with nothing on underneath. Here I also felt stripped of my privileged position as a doctor. At the third gate, I entered the labor room, to lie on my back for the vaginal examinations that were done regularly to check how quickly and how much my cervix was dilating and thus how far along in labor I was. As labor continued, I incrementally lost the sense of being in control. It felt as if I were in the underworld, in an altered state of consciousness. I felt waves of pain that crested and receded, each wave becoming longer and more intense, with shorter and shorter intervals of rest in between. This was hard, painful physical work, building toward some crescendo that felt increasingly unbearable. The pain at some point was so bad that the intervals in between became filled with anticipatory fear. Then, I got a paracervical block, which consists of shots of a novocaine-like anesthesia that numbs the cervix area and takes the edge off the pain. Somewhere in the midst of this—I've lost track of when it was—I was wheeled through another gate into the delivery room.

The period just before delivery itself, when labor pains are the most intense and the longest, is called "transition." It's when the baby moves through the cervix into the foreshortened birth canal, passing under the mother's pubic arch to emerge into the world. And it's when the mother feels most like giving up because the ordeal is just too much, like a marathon runner hitting "the wall" just before the end of the race; it's a situation when more is called for from the body than the mind knows is possible. But where will carries the runner on, the last throes of labor are beyond will and choice; there is only surrender to what is happening in and to you. Once in the midst of transition, labor continues until it is over, ending in the birth of a baby, or, as we know somewhere in our depths from time immemorial, in the death of the mother.

This is the crucial liminal time for both baby and mother, when the baby literally goes through a gateway into the next phase, when the danger of damage to baby and mother are the greatest. This is the prototype of all life transitions: once we go through the passage, nothing is the same.

And so it was. With one last push, my baby came through me into the world. I was now the gate myself. Shortly thereafter I heard a cry and was told I'd had a girl and that she was fine. She was wrapped and momentarily put in my arms, evoking mother-tenderness immediately, and amazement that this little person had grown inside of me.

In the midst of labor and delivery, so much was going on; so much became known to me in an unfamiliar way, without words or thinking. One more time, with the birth of my son sixteen months later, I reentered this initiation. Again I participated in a women's mystery and had something revealed to me that I think of as a diffusion rather than an illumination. It was like descending downward into the dark, dissolving into it, and then knowing. This way contrasts with that moment of clarity, that split-second revelation that comes like lightning, an illumination when the mind suddenly knows. The "I" that had accomplished things in the world was not in the labor or delivery room. This was an initiation, through which I experienced a profound kinship with all women throughout history who had ever gone through this ordeal and transformation. There was nothing that distinguished me from any woman anywhere who had ever given birth to a baby.

The experience of labor and delivery recruited me into the women's movement. Kinship with women, deep sisterhood, began there. I had a mystical sense of oneness with all women through time. None of my accomplishments mattered or set me apart, my individuality meant nothing. In this experience, I was everywoman, anywoman, Woman. This was a profound revelation.

I could contrast my own experience of medical school and the rite of passage of internship, which were at that time among the major initiation ordeals for men, with having just had a baby. In many ways, having a baby was harder; certainly the need to surrender to the experience was absolute. Under the most positive of circumstances, with all my knowledge of what was happening and the support from my husband, doctor, and the nursing staff, there was still the pain and fear and the isolation of being the one in whom it was all happening. I could appreciate how in pregnancy, labor, and delivery, women everywhere go through a major rite of passage that is not acknowledged as such by us, by society, or by religions. In male rites of passage, the elements of ordeal, risk of death, and transformation are enacted (for example, in fraternity hazing and initiations into gang membership, as well as in aboriginal rituals described by anthropologists; through such rites, manhood is defined). What is only enacted in male ceremony is the literal situation in pregnancy: labor *is* an ordeal, there *is* an inherent risk of death, the woman *is* transformed. In the process of this initiation, a maiden's body becomes a mother's, and she gives birth to new life. Yet this is just the beginning of her commitment; for the child to survive and thrive, the initiate must be responsible for this new life. While she alone is not responsible for the continuation of the human species, the human species continues because one lone woman at a time goes through this initiation and brings new life through her.

Pregnancy was for me a profound experience with sacred moments and awful ones. It was a rite of passage and an experience that changed me forever.

When I looked back on my medical training, I was appalled at what I had taken part in by not recognizing and not protesting the callousness and derogatory attitudes I saw expressed (and to a lesser extent, felt myself) toward women who "behaved badly" in labor at the three county hospitals where I trained. I recall incidents: the young woman who screamed in pain and fear as labor intensified, who was told by an obstetrical resident, "You should have thought about this when you spread your legs." I remember the contempt that was voiced by house staff at hearing women beseeching the Virgin for help, and the times they were mocked for it. In the delivery rooms, medical students and interns did the normal deliveries, and it was often obvious that this was a learning experience. Yet these were better situations, I might add, than many others that I have heard of from other physicians who've told me what they witnessed in their training. My own pregnancy also convinced me that no woman should be made to go through this against her will, especially if conception came about due to rape or incest—circumstances that desecrated her body and soul.

A pregnant woman surrenders to the process of the pregnancy, labor, and delivery. She will be transformed through the experience that affects her body and psyche. The focus, however, is not on the woman but on the baby she is carrying: we anticipate the birth of the child and wonder who the newborn will be. Equally significant as a potential new birth is who the woman will become as a result of this experience.

Pregnancy is like the creativity that comes from making a descent into one's own depth, in which the person is changed in the process of bringing forth the work—creative work that comes out of the soul and is the child of it. This experience of pregnancy and this process of creativity can be symbolized by the labyrinth found near the entrances to ritual caves and on the floors of cathedrals, which are womb-like spaces.

Deepening the Experience of the Mother: Breastfeeding as Sacred Communion

As I recall nursing, I do more than bring the experience to mind. My breasts remember and I become aware of sensation in them. My body is an organ of memory as well as perception.

Breastfeeding was a mixed experience for me, because "I" (my body) didn't make an abundance of milk. I wasn't a font. And so there were times when my breasts were full and times when they were not. During the day, breastfeeding often felt like work that I wasn't good enough at. The early morning feeding was the time of fullness.

That early morning (4:00 A.M.) feeding was also an extraordinary experience of oneness and stillness and communion and symbiosis. We lived in an apartment in Sausalito that looked out over San Francisco Bay. I would sit in a rocker in the dark, nursing my infant with my breasts full of milk. Then and still later, with this content child cradled in my arms, I was one with my baby and with the night and with the bay.

Stephanie Demetrakopoulos, in *Listening to Our Bodies: The Rebirth of Feminine Wisdom*, speaks eloquently for women for whom breastfeeding is an even more central experience than it was for me when she recalls the feelings she had when nursing her two children:

> The psychic longing for both of them was sometimes unbearable. The accumulation of breast-milk and the pent-up desire for them particularly echoed each other. This longing and the relief at being with my children again constitute some of the deepest passions I have experienced. The older the child, the less acute that longing; but it is a commingling of psyche and body in feminine yearning and love that is highly specific to the mother-child bond.

Demetrakopoulos (whose Greek name is an echo of Demeter the mother goddess) also tells of a profound maternal experience that occurred through nursing a child that was not her own:

> One orphan that I learned to care about was a Down's syndrome infant. When nursing my last child, I was asked by a foster mother, a friend of mine, to nurse this infant who had been given up at birth by his mother. The baby was allergic to formula and needed breast milk to heal his very raw diaper rash. Nursing this little boy was gratifying and fulfilling in a different way from nursing my own children; the impersonal *caritas* (affection, care, grace) of giving to this little waif put me in touch with a new aspect of the Goddess. . . . This experience (six years ago) has had a remarkable effect on my fantasy life. When I feel especially joyful and loving toward the world, the memory of that infant sometimes comes to me, not as a visual image,

but as a tactile image. I feel him in my arms and smell his aroma; sometimes I even sense the milk dropping.

She was reminded of the seventeenth-century Catholic depiction of the Virgin Mary standing in heaven and streaming milk as divine grace down onto the world. Her experience reminded me of the cup and the words of communion. A nursing woman putting a child to her breast is expressing, without words, "Take, eat, this is my body; drink, this is my blood." For it is literally out of her body and her blood that a woman's milk is made. We and all life on the Earth are like nursing infants. Mother Earth sustains and nourishes us; everything we need comes out of the body and atmosphere of Gaia. We eat and drink of her.

Demetrakopoulos maintains that the knowledge gained from breastfeeding is not a passing one, but a reference point in the consciousness of women for their whole lives. I believe that this is so *only* if there are words to describe it as well—words that describe previously inarticulate experience, recall the experience, and make it a part of what we know.

I am also struck with how often women *sense* in their bodies, especially in the breast and heart area, when they are giving, loving, and responding to the needs of others. Demetrakopoulos quotes a psychic friend of hers, who made the following analogy: "When I feel that someone needs healing, the divine energy flows up into the heart and breast area. I can only describe this as like being at a party three miles away when your breasts fill and you know the baby's hungry. The urgency to get home and feed it is like wanting to heal someone who needs it." She notes that this is like nursing on a spiritual level, in which both the healer and the one needing healing feel relief and serenity, one from the release of pent-up love and the other from receiving its flow.

Women's Experience of the Blood Mysteries

Once I understood how my pregnancy had been an initiation, I mused further upon menarche, menstruation, and menopause, as "blood mysteries." In patriarchy, flow and cessation of uterine blood is either an unmentionable or shameful subject; menstruation is referred to as "the curse." In the Old Testament a menstruating woman is considered unclean; a menopausal woman has gone through a change that lessens her. How would it be different if the fertility of earth and women were celebrated as expressions of divinity and if women elders were appreciated as wisewomen?

At puberty, when a girl made the physical transition into womanhood, her body changing shape, she would know that she was beginning to resemble the Goddess. The beginning of menses, her first bleeding time, would be celebrated. Blood would be held in awe. This blood would mean that she could now become fertile, that she could be like the Goddess or the Earth, and life could come forth from her.

Her cyclical bleeding time, like the menstrual periods of women who live together in dormitories or sororities, would occur at the same time as for other menstruating women, and they would all be in synchrony with a phase of the moon, a living testament to the connection between women and Nature. She would bleed every month, except when she became pregnant. For these nine months, it could be said that she retained the blood in her body to make a baby. Throughout her fertile years, this would be so, until at menopause she once again stopped bleeding. And perhaps this would be considered even more awesome; for now it could be said that she retained the blood in her body to make wisdom.

Every woman would thus be an embodiment of the Goddess who was celebrated in her three aspects, as Maiden, Mother, and Crone, each phase also being an expression of the blood mysteries that defined the woman.

Women have within their bodies a mysterious hidden womb, an organ of creativity, nurturing, and fertility, and a symbol of the creative, fertile, and nourishing feminine principle, as are breasts. Images of these once-sacred symbols were destroyed as graven images or buried. They are being dug up at archaeological sites, and they are emerging in the psyches of women, unearthed from the unconscious through active imagination or dream images.

Women's mysteries, the blood mysteries of the body, are not the same as the physical realities of menstruation, lactation, pregnancy, and menopause; for physiology to become mystery, a mystical affiliation must be made between a woman and the archetypal feminine. A woman must

68

sense, know, or imagine herself as Woman, as Goddess, as an embodiment of the feminine principle. The examples I have used in this chapter illustrate this connection between a woman's body and her awareness or discovery of this mystery. Under patriarchy, this connection has been suppressed; there are no words or rituals that celebrate the connection between a woman's physiological initiations and spiritual meaning.

Not only can I imagine it being different when God was a woman as in Old Europe twenty thousand years ago, it is also different when Native Americans recover the traditions that the United States government and the Church tried to destroy through taking all Indian youngsters into church-run residential schools designed to subvert and convert heathens. I recall hearing a Navajo woman psychiatrist tell about celebrating her daughter's menarche. It was the first time that I could imagine how different girls could feel about menstruation and the significance of it and the pride and self-respect that could come from having such traditions. I contrasted it with how the onset of menstruation is observed by shame-based or scientific-minded families. Daughters are unprepared and shocked by the onset of bleeding "down there," clandestinely informed and given pads, or shown diagrams in books or films on the physiology of menstruation.

Women's mysteries are of the body *and* the psyche. A woman may go through the physical experiences that comprise the blood mysteries but miss the soul dimension of being a woman entirely; or she may experience the sacred dimension of the Goddess as an aspect of herself or as coming through her or may have her creativity or wisdom shaped by being in a woman's body but be a celibate, or never be pregnant, or have a surgical menopause.

A woman does not have to be a biological mother in order to be an initiate into the maternal aspect of the Goddess; it comes through her own embodied maternal and feminine nature—through which she feels her kinship with women, with animals, and with Nature. Her psyche resides in her body and her wisdom grows out of an instinctual knowledge of what to do with her hands and body to soothe, to comfort, or take charge of a situation that calls upon this in her: she responds to a woman in labor, an animal with a paw in a trap, a woman in hysterical grief, a terrified child too young to understand what is happening with a maternal authority that others instinctively recognize. When she takes charge by doing whatever needs to be done, Mother has arrived.

A woman may instinctively provide a psychological womb space for others. She may do this in a helping or teaching profession or as a spouse, mother, or friend: in whatever the circumstance, whatever the other person brings to her that is undeveloped, fragile, and vulnerable is held and positively nourished by her attitude and belief in the capacity of the person to grow.

A woman may also give birth to her own creative work, which comes out of the womb of her own experience in which she has had to plumb her own depth as a woman and labor to bring it forth. A woman who does this gives herself over to a creative process that is like a pregnancy, when this is the case. Something in her wants to be given form through her; the work comes out of her and draws from her talents and experience, and yet it has its own life.

A woman who is maternal, nurturing, or creative in these ways does not live in her head. There is an instinctual feminine quality to what she does and how she does what she does, or knows what she knows.

Just as a woman may surrender her body to be a vessel in pregnancy, in some similar invisible way mediumistic women can become the chalice through which consciousness may emerge. The sybils, Delphic Oracles, and Native American women who had dreams for the tribe functioned in this way. These psychic women commonly had to lose consciousness for the dream or information to come through them, a parallel to women who are anesthetized during labor and delivery. Both experiences change when consciousness is not surrendered, and a woman is aware of the awesomeness and privilege of what it is she does. She is now a chosen vessel and she herself has made the choice of what she is doing with her body or psyche. She taps into archetypal depths or biological depths that mysteriously come together in soul experiences and is conscious of being this chalice through which life or vision emerges. At this particular time, many women are birthing Goddess consciousness.

In the Arms of the Goddess

When I felt the presence of God at age eighteen, it was ineffable and real, and there was context for it. I was at a Christian summer camp, people were speaking of God and praying to Him, so I knew what the experience was. I could define it for myself and to others. The year I turned forty, I had another numinous experience. I now know that this experience was of the Goddess. By contrast, I had no context to help me name what this was.

It happened in my office toward the end of an analytic hour with a woman who, under other circumstances, could easily have been my friend. In analysis, she had moved into a major creative period in her life. And on that day, I was more tired than I knew. I was weary and full of unexpressed grief.

A week before, a patient of mine had been found dead under suspicious circumstances. The period before her death had been a good one for her, and I had seen her on the day she died. That evening, the coroner's office called me with the news, which I had to break to others. In the intervening week, I had been in touch with the staff at the day treatment center where she had been, had spent a session with her son who was still a youngster, and had had several contacts with one of her closest friends, who was also my patient. And when no other possibilities were forthcoming, I had arranged with a priest I knew at Grace Cathedral to do a memorial service there. Meanwhile, I had other patients, my teaching, and my responsibilities as wife and mother to deal with.

No one supposed I needed any comforting, including me, until this woman who was my analysand sensed something and reached out with compassion to ask if I was all right. And when my eyes moistened with sudden tears, she broke out of role, got out of the patient's chair to come over to mine, and held me. At that moment, I felt that a much larger presence was there with the two of us. When this woman put her arms around me, I felt as if we were both being cradled in the arms of an invisible, divine presence. I was profoundly comforted and felt a deep ache in the center of my chest. This was before I had ever heard of a heart chakra, which I know now opened widely then.

I now also know that this is a way that the Goddess (of whom I had no inkling) may manifest. It differed from the mystical experience I had had of God. Then, no other human presence was necessary, and prayer provided a sense of continuity and connection.

Here, in contrast, the compassion and arms of a woman were the means through which a numinous maternal presence was felt. I felt deeply comforted, as if body and soul were held in the arms of female divinity that was larger than us both. It was a transpersonal experience as was my experience of God, but it had a physical component, "God" was transcendent—as if from above and of the spirit; "Goddess" came through a human woman in a moment of loving compassion and left me with an aching deep quiet place in my heart, as a body imprint. Like the experience of God, this sacred moment of the Goddess was ineffable, arose when I was vulnerable, and occurred in a sacred place. For the "analytic container" is every bit as special a place as a chapel, in being a *temenos,* the Greek word for "sanctuary"; and it differs in having therapy boundaries and therapeutic goals. In this space, what happened between us needed to be analyzed and understood, and at that time the intellectual tools of transference and countertransference were all that I had to work with. I did the best I knew then, but efforts to reduce the experience to this were not adequate.

It had a lasting effect: from that point on, whenever I was moved by compassion for anyone, I'd feel an upwelling of love, accompanied by a now-familiar ache in my heart chakra, in the center of my chest between my breasts. This would be where I would also later feel that tuning-fork response, first at Chartres Cathedral and then at other sacred sites. It's a rapport I feel in my body.

I now think of this profound moment as a Grail experience in which the Goddess was the Grail that held us. This, and what others have told me about their experiences of the Goddess in their lives, has made me think of the Goddess as a nurturer and comforter whose presence is evoked through human touch.

Once I became aware that women can feel the presence of the Goddess as a maternal, feminine, deeply comforting energy, I could recognize what two women reported as happening in a cave in Montana, as a goddess experience.

They were part of a women's wisdom workshop that I was leading. We had entered a ritual cave in which human artifacts had been found dating back to the Ice Age. A cave is a symbolic womb and tomb; to descend into it is to enact a symbolic journey into the earth, the underworld, and the otherworld, the place from which all life comes and to which all life returns in death. It is the mythological realm of the Greek goddess Persephone and the earlier Sumerian goddess Erishkigal. Our group numbered about forty. Using flashlights we entered the cave; each woman kept the woman in front of her and behind her within touching distance as we walked, sometimes stooping to get through a low place, moving mostly downward, helping each other wherever the footing became difficult, traversing a lengthy labyrinthine route that opened up into a large chamber where we sat around a rock altar formation. A candle was the only illumination. It was like being together in a womb of the Earth, in a comforting place of darkness.

Any woman who had entered menopause, either through age or surgery, could participate in her own initiation as wisewoman by stepping forward, picking up the candle, and speaking. Each who chose to told us what she had learned, the wisdom she had gained through living her particular life.

Clare spoke about her hysterectomy, which had ended her deep desire to bear a child. She told us of the estrangement she had felt from her own mother, which healed when her mother came to be with her while she recuperated from surgery. It could happen only because Clare had followed her intuition and had asked her mother to come. A middle child in a very large family, she had never before been the only concern of her mother. She had arrived at forgiveness for the neglect she had experienced as a child, and a new bond between them had been forged, but the grief and pain that she could never be a mother herself remained. She spoke of it, put the candle down, and returned tearfully to where she had been seated. The woman next to her opened her arms and held her, and in that moment, she too felt embraced as I once had, not just by a woman but by the Goddess who comes through women, as a numinous, comforting, healing presence.

The next time I experienced the Goddess come to comfort a woman in this way was in a great stone circle in Ireland. I had led a guided meditation, during which a woman named Patricia relived the time when she first went away from home to go to camp and returned to find that in her absence her mother had given her beloved dog to the garbage man. Grief and disbelief were written across her face as if it had just happened and she were only seven. Jo, who was sitting next to her, responded with compassion and spontaneously reached out to comfort her; whether it was with her arms, as Patricia remembers, or her words and heart, as Jo recollects, Patricia felt herself held and comforted by a mother presence that was numinous and healing. Jo also felt that she was participating in something extraordinary and had an awareness that the two of them were in a "powerfully charged ovoid space" or energy field.

Jo wrote to me of what she perceived and did.

The meditation ended; people sat up, stood up, and began to walk away. Patricia seemed immobilized, she was still seated, her head and shoulders falling forward. I hooked into the immediacy of the energy and said, 'Patricia, I'll hold you in my heart while you do what you need to do.' She moved deeper into the well of grief, turning to lie on the ground, crying. I sat next to her, holding with my heart the holy space for her. I felt like everything I've done in my life—my own experience with grief, my experience with others in therapy—all brought me perfectly to this moment.

As the tide of Patricia's energy seemed to pass the ebb, and then to flow back in, she stood up and started slow tai chi–like movements. I stood up too, and we filled our ovoid space with dance, gathering in the ecstasy of completion. Surely, indeed, the Goddess was present.

In these moments, when each of us felt held in the arms of the Mother Goddess, a compassionate woman mediated the experience, leading me to understand that this feminine divinity comes through the body and heart of a human woman, created in Her image.

All of the blood mysteries I have described so far are archetypally those of Persephone-Demeter-Hecate, the maiden-mother-crone, each an aspect of the Triple Goddess, the three faces of the feminine. There is one other blood mystery initiation: the deflowering of the maiden, who bleeds when her hymen is broken. When it is a Persephone experience, no matter how much consent a

woman may give with her heart and mind, there is resistance at the body level. The maiden experiences a violation
of her physical or psychological virginity; her intactness has
been broken, and she feels taken or possessed. She is a de-
flowered, abducted Persephone who may become a pregnant Demeter.

A young woman who is archetypally Aphrodite, however, can respond to a passionate and sensitive lover with
her whole body when she is penetrated the first time. The
small amount of bleeding that stains the sheets is then a
sign of the embodied initiation that transformed her from
a sexually unawakened maiden into a sexual woman,
which is a sacred mystery. When both lovers are moved
from within by Aphrodite, intercourse can become a communion celebrated at the body-soul level. That sexual
union can be a sacramental act through which divinity
comes is, for patriarchal religion, literally beyond belief.

As with every blood mystery, the physical experience
needs to have a sacred component in order for it to initiate a
woman. A woman is not automatically transformed from
uninitiated maiden to knowing woman by losing her virginity. The transformative mystery of Aphrodite, goddess of
love and beauty, whom I called the "alchemical goddess" in
Goddesses in Everywoman, may be the least experienced
women's mystery in patriarchy. It is a mystery that women
are more likely to be initiated into later in life, if at all.

In traditional patriarchy, a woman's body belongs to her
husband and is to be responsive to his needs, not her own.

Desire having to do with the body is "carnal," "sinful," and, for women, not to be enjoyed. For two thousand years, there has been a madonna-whore split: women who enjoyed their sexuality were "whores." Repression of sexuality kept women safe; a "good woman" was socially protected, married, and a mother.

When the male is supposed to be the dominator, a man's human and divine potential as ecstatic lover is also inhibited, though he may become proficient as a lover and be proud of his skillfulness, which he has learned and practiced. To experience the Goddess through the body of a human woman, his ego cannot be in control of her or himself. Love rather than power must be present for the Goddess to be present in this embodied Mystery.

Just as a pregnant woman or a woman who puts her infant to her breast can enter an altered state of consciousness and be aware that she is participating in a sacred moment in which she and the mother goddess are one, so is it possible to experience being in a sacramental lovemaking experience in which the woman and Aphrodite the goddess are one.

Women's Mysteries and the Grail

We must remember how and when each of us has had an experience of the Goddess, and felt healed and made whole by her. These are holy, sacred, timeless moments, and as numinous as they may have been, without words they are difficult to retrieve. But when someone else speaks of a similar experience, it can evoke the memory and bring back the feelings, which restores the experience. Only if we speak from personal experience does this happen. This is why we need words for women's mysteries, which, like everything else that is of women, seems to require that one woman at a time birth what she knows. We serve as midwives to each other's consciousness. To speak our own truth the first time feels fraught with danger. It becomes easier each time. In the bones of our collective experience as women we know there are risks.

Somewhere in our souls, we remember the burning time, when women were persecuted and burned alive as witches. This went on for three hundred years of the Inquisition. In what has been referred to in contemporary times as "the women's holocaust," more women were burned at the stake than were killed in the Nazi gas ovens during the Holocaust in World War II. First the midwives were burned for easing the pains of childbirth (which went against the biblical injunction that women were supposed to suffer), then the healers who knew the medicinal uses of herbs, women who celebrated the seasons, eccentric women, women with possessions someone coveted, outspoken women, bright women, women without protection. This collective memory has an effect much as any personal repressed trauma does; it makes women anxious when we discover our own sacred experiences and find words for them. We need courage to bring forth what we know.

Somewhere in our souls, women remember a time when divinity was called Goddess and Mother. When we become initiates into women's mysteries we then come to know that we are the carriers of a holy chalice, that the Grail comes through us.

SIX

Pilgrimage to Glastonbury

Pilgrimages invite reflection. We become as receptive to our own thoughts, feelings, and memories as we are to the impressions we receive at sacred sites. As a result, we muse, recollect significant experiences, and make connections, much as I have been doing in the last two chapters. Then, when we arrive at the next place on our itinerary, we once more shift attention outward. On this particular pilgrimage the route I was taking was as labyrinthine at the beginning as the labyrinth at Chartres.

I had gone from the Netherlands, where I met the Dalai Lama, to Chartres, and then I turned around and went back to Holland before setting out on the next part of the pilgrimage, which was to Glastonbury, England. Mrs. Detiger had arranged for me to have a companion on this part of the journey who would be meeting me in the Netherlands, and we would embark to Glastonbury from there.

While I had never been to either place, Chartres Cathedral had somehow been clearly established as a real place in my mind. Glastonbury was something else again; for me it was more a mythological place than a geographical one.

Glastonbury

Mrs. Detiger's invitation had been emphatic: "You must go to Glastonbury." Her certainty, not to mention the timing of her letter, contributed to my feeling that this was no ordinary invitation. For she could not have known that this was a destination that I myself had been drawn to by a dream that I had had many years earlier, a place that had captivated my imagination since reading *The Mists of Avalon*. In this novel, Glastonbury was the place where one crossed through the mists to Avalon, the last realm of the Goddess where women were priestesses, healers, and visionaries.

Glastonbury is actually a small town in Somerset, in the western part of England. The town surrounds a forty-acre rectangle, on which still exist a few impressive ruins of Glastonbury Abbey, once the greatest church in England. The most notable feature is an unusual hill with a tower on its top, on the outskirts of the town. This is Glastonbury Tor, which rises 518 feet above sea level.

Glastonbury is surrounded by a wide expanse of low-lying fields. From the Tor, one sees a gentle landscape with soft contours and cultivated greenness. From afar, the Tor rises sharply above the fields out of a cluster of hills, giving it the air of an island. The flat region that extends westward toward the Bristol Channel and the sea was once covered with water. Boats would have docked alongside what are now hills; traces of a wharf have been found at Wearyall Hill.

Wearyall Hill is so named, according to the Christian contributions to Glastonbury legend, because this is where Joseph of Arimathea and his companions from the Holy Land came ashore, weary all from the long journey. On disembarking, Joseph, who in the New Testament provided the tomb for the crucified Jesus, purportedly drove his staff into the ground, where it miraculously came to life as a tree. This tree, called the Holy Thorn, blossomed every Christmas. While this tree was destroyed, its descendants in Glastonbury still bloom during late December and early January. A sprig of the Holy Thorn's winter blossom is even now sent annually to the reigning English sovereign. The Holy Thorn is unique among English trees, resembling most closely a tree that grows in or near the Holy Land.

Glastonbury is a center of Celtic, Arthurian, Christian, and esoteric legend and history. Geoffrey Ashe's books (especially *Avalonian Quest*) provide the most useful perspective on the many claims made about Glastonbury: that it was venerated as the holiest place in Britain before Christianity and was the site of the first Christian community; that Joseph of Arimathea came there with the Holy Grail from the Last Supper, which was afterward lost; that the Tor and hill cluster that cradles Glastonbury was once the Isle of Avalon, where Arthur was taken wounded after his last battle; that it is one of the great energy centers of the Western world.

And now here I was on my way to Glastonbury, this place that had been in the back of my mind for more than twenty years, ever since I had had the following dream:

I was going down a dimly lit, narrow, secret spiral stairway that led beneath a cathedral to a hidden room. The room was airy and spacious and filled with light. In it was the body of a knight or a king in armor. He had been dead for centuries and yet looked as he had in life (like Snow White did after she took a bite of the poisoned apple). He wore a ring with a large oval green or bluish stone, which was now given to me to wear. Then I was in the basement of a very large department store. It was as if I had gone through the wall of the room under the cathedral and emerged into this bustling, ordinary place. I was wearing the ring but had turned the stone so that it was hidden inside my cupped hand where only I could see it. Only a plain band showed outwardly.

This was a significant dream in which I discovered that an Arthurian knight or king was hidden below the church floor. He was a symbol of masculine authority, spirituality, strength, courage, and honor, and for me to have received and worn his ring on my right ring finger meant that I was to be true to or carry what he represented into the world. Yet because the stone would be immediately noticed and give away something that I was to keep secret, I had to turn the ring so that the stone was hidden from view.

When I recounted the dream to my Jungian analyst, he asked me if I had ever heard of Glastonbury Abbey (which I had not). I imagine that he knew that the remains thought to be King Arthur had been found beneath the abbey grounds. He also mentioned a book that he had come across many years before called *The Gate of Remembrance*. Both Glastonbury and the book title stayed with me over the years, as do things that carry a sense of mystery. At the time of the dream I tried to locate the book and could find no trace of its existence.

I have been reminded of this dream many times over the years and have had several related dreams as well. Here is another dream from the same period:

> I am in a medieval building made of stone, with a cloister and an inner court area. I go into a small room off the cloister, where the wall pivots open—like a secret

wall in a mystery film—and I am now outdoors, in a Sunday-at-the-park setting, with lots of picnicking people who have no way of knowing that just a moment before I was in a different world.

It's no wonder that *The Mists of Avalon* would intrigue me, for my own dreams pointed to the possibility of crossing from one reality to another. Also, considering that I could dream of an Arthurian knight and of wearing his ring out into the world, it's not surprising that when I set out on this journey I could so readily identify with Perceval. As for Glastonbury itself, I would find that it was like entering a dream landscape that was imbued with legends and stories, including the claim that this is a place where the veil is thinner.

Sighting the Tor

To get to Glastonbury, we drove west from Heathrow Airport on a highway that took us past Stonehenge. Several smaller roads later and we were on the Shepton Mallet Road, a narrow and not particularly straight road bordered by hedgerows and fences. The road took us through fields in which sheep grazed and through part of the disputed Glastonbury Zodiac, whose proponents declare that Glastonbury lies within a Zodiac Circle roughly ten miles across, the figures of which are formed by features in the landscape that are supposedly in the same relative positions as the constellations in the sky.

Suddenly the road changed—it could have been a shift in angle or elevation, or a gap in the hedgerow—and there was Glastonbury Tor! I say this with an exclamation point, because that is the impact; it is something to behold. The Tor is a mountain that is really only a hill, except that calling it a hill would not do it justice. It was lushly green and apparently terraced, with a sentinel tower on its summit. Since it was late May, there were apple trees in bloom near its base and in the fields nearby. From the initial vantage point, the Tor looked triangular in shape, like a pyramid. Then, as the road took us past it, its outline changed, as the angle of one slope elongated.

From any angle, the Tor emanates power and mystery. There is something unnatural and sculptural about its shape, with its spiral terraces that appear to wind around its sides and the tower on the top that looks like a Stonehenge-sized megalith. The tower is the only remaining part of a Saint Michael's Church that once dominated the Tor. An uncommon earthquake collapsed the church and left only the tower standing.

In England, places that were once sacred to the Goddess were taken over by Christians in one of two ways: by building churches named for Saint Michael, as on the Tor, or chapels in honor of Mary. Saint Michael is usually portrayed stamping upon a serpent, which was a symbol of the Goddess, and one that also expresses the telluric energy currents or ley lines (as they are called in England) that "snake" under the ground at sacred sites. In China, these lines are known as *lung-mei,* the paths of the dragon; to this day in modern Hong Kong, Chinese geomancers are consulted about these dragon currents before buildings are constructed.

Areas where the energy is strongest became sacred sites or, in current idiom, power points. The images that are associated with this energy are archetypally similar, whether you're in Western Europe or China. The snake and the Chinese dragon and the serpent all have undulating bodies and power. But whereas in a culture that respected the Earth the dragon was thought of as benevolent, in Judeo-Christian cultures where the Earth (and goddesses and women) had to be tamed and subjugated, dragons, snakes, and serpents were to be feared—stamped out by Saint Michael, driven out by Saint Patrick, or killed by Saint George.

It amused me to think that the earthquake that knocked down Saint Michael's Abbey from the Tor might have been an expression of an offended Mother Earth Goddess who refused to be downtrodden. Saint Michael prevailed, however, for the Saint Michael's Abbey that was once on the Tor is one of many that still stand, located on a ley line that runs down the spine of southwest England to the island rock of Saint Michael's Mound near Land's End, Cornwall.

The second way of usurping goddess sites was by building chapels or cathedrals in honor of Mary on them. As a feminine expression of divinity, Mary is archetypally the mother goddess. In all but name, this is how she is worshiped at Chartres, for example. For regardless of discriminating points made by theologians, the man or woman who prays to Mary is speaking to the same compassionate goddess whose names were, among others, Demeter, Isis, Tara, or Kuan Yin, goddesses who, like Mary, understood suffering. Demeter's daughter Persephone was abducted into the underworld and Isis's son Osiris was torn to pieces. Like Mary's crucified son, both Persephone and Osiris were resurrected. When Mary chapels are built on old goddess sites, they are, in effect, reconsecrated and renamed, places where it can be said that the Goddess continues to be honored.

The road took us past Glastonbury Tor toward the town, to Chalice Hill House where we would stay. On arriving, I found that Geoffrey Ashe, author and expert on the history and legends of the area, was waiting, a meeting that Mrs. Detiger had arranged. He took us up to where we could get a panoramic view of the area and discern in the landscape the figure of a reclining woman. Later Barri Devigne, a lifelong Arthurian scholar, took us to Cadbury, the probable site of Camelot. On the way, he stopped to point out specific features of the Glastonbury Zodiac. To look at the landscape and see what they were seeing was like looking at the constellations in the nighttime sky; the landmarks are easy to make out, as are the stars when someone locates them for us, but not so obvious are the figures of which they are a part. At Glastonbury, the landscape evokes imagination, inviting people to see beyond ordinary reality.

Walking the Tor

My first morning in Glastonbury, I arose early and took a walk by myself from Chalice Hill House past apple trees in bloom and up the slopes of the Tor. At that hour, I was the only person there. The spiral terraces, which look so well defined from afar and are supposed to number seven, were not at all easy to follow once I began the climb. As I had walked the labyrinth at Chartres Cathedral, now I wanted to walk the Tor. And as I made my way on these spirals up to the top, the experience felt puzzling and somehow wrong.

When one views the Tor from afar, the tower commands attention and seems to be the destination toward which spiraling paths go. On the Tor itself, however—as I subjectively sensed the place and let images arise in reaction to being there, which I had done at Chartres Cathedral—I had several impressions. The tower now felt like an imposed structure, an artifact that did not belong. Instead, it felt to me that power resided in this uterine-shaped mountain itself. And rather than having an impulse to go up to the summit, I felt that there should have been a tunnel going into the mountain from below.

These thoughts, I later found, turned out to be age-old conjectures that others have shared about the Tor: Might it have a hollow place within it? Might the Tor have an entrance to the underworld? Geoffrey Ashe writes, "To this day there is a stubborn local legend that the Tor has a chamber inside it. Usually the chamber is said to be below the summit, perhaps a considerable distance below. People are alleged to have found a way in and come out mad."

In Celtic mythology, the otherworld, underground realm is Annwn, a faerie realm. This realm has been associated with Glastonbury Tor. In Annwn, there was a magical cauldron of plenty that unceasingly provided wonderful nourishment. This cauldron was either the same as or interchangeable with the magical cauldron of rebirth and regeneration, in which the dead could be recreated, made new, and reborn. I see the cauldron and the Grail as symbolically related, for in some versions of the Grail story, the Grail is a vessel that provides whatever food the person desires. Also, as a symbol of Jesus and the Last Supper, the Grail is connected with his death and resurrection and the promise of eternal life. His three days in the tomb would correspond to being in the underworld in the cauldron of rebirth and regeneration.

Tunnels and hollow underground places are images that are universally connected with Mother Earth as womb and tomb, with the Goddess who gives us life and takes us back in death. The Earth certainly functions as a cauldron of regeneration: everything dies and goes into either the earth or the earth's atmosphere and is recycled and regenerated into new life. Mother Earth is also the cauldron of plenty, out of which comes everything needed to nourish life.

The uterine-shaped Glastonbury Tor evokes thoughts about the underworld and hidden spaces underground.

Walking the Tor, images and feelings arose in me that correspond to myths and legends long held about the place. On this first visit to Glastonbury, I was unaware of these stories about the Tor. I wonder now: Is there an underground realm there, or does the shape of the Tor conjure up the image? What is it about the Tor, anyway? For it seems that whether in the depth of the earth or in the depth of our psyches, images connected to the otherworld and to the Goddess come into the consciousness of visitor and native alike.

For me, walking the Tor and forming impressions that turned out to be part of legend and conjecture fit with what has been said about Glastonbury: it is indeed a place where the veil between the worlds is thinner. Here images came into my mind that related to belief held about the Tor, and my body seemed to sense that I was not following an ancient ritual path, when I assumed that there was a spiral path to the summit. Not only did it "feel wrong," it also isn't possible to walk such a path without occasionally having to scramble from one level to another.

After much study and walking the Tor, Geoffrey Ashe concluded that there is a path and that it is in the shape of a Cretan labyrinth (see figure). At Glastonbury as at Chartres the labyrinth is present. This one is a three-dimensional, simpler version, whose path follows the pattern of a Cretan labyrinth, which is the most common shape for a labyrinth. Such labyrinths are found carved into the rock of caves in many parts of the world. I thus was walking on a three-dimensional version of the more

elegant and symmetrical two-dimensional labyrinth at Chartres, and at both sites, the labyrinth evoked an image of the womb. I saw the Tor as uterine-shaped and the labyrinth at Chartres positioned where the uterus would be in the body of the cathedral.

If these impressions were true, then, in the language of *The Mists of Avalon*, they would be examples of the gift of Sight—a way of knowing that may come naturally to many or most women, as do spatial abilities for many or most men. In any case, intuitive or extrasensory ways of knowing are not given much credit in our culture.

I think a good parallel can be found in the experience of house hunting. On walking into empty houses readied for sale, or even into a particular room of a house, we often seem to *sense* whether memories here are happy, sad, or even dreadful. And sometimes when we ask, our realtor provides some information that makes it likely that our impression is correct. This falls into the parapsychological category of psychometry; it's what a psychic does when she picks up an object and describes the owner.

Psychometry and the possibility that there are morphic fields, as theoretical biologist Rupert Sheldrake has proposed, account for and explain how it might be possible for us to go to an archaeological, historic, or sacred site and get a true impression of what happened there in the past. Sheldrake describes morphic fields as a source of cumulative memory based upon experiences of a species in the past. The human morphic field is what we tap into and are resonating with and influenced by when we respond as members of the human race, doing what humans have done. From prehistoric to contemporary times, humans have held spiritual beliefs, observed rituals, had places of worship, and related to divinity. Whatever the particular practice or place, whatever spiritual or mystical experience humans have had is in some way contained within the morphic fields of our species, the contents of which span time and distance. Sheldrake's morphic resonance theory (as applied to humans) and Jung's concept of the collective unconscious are very similar ideas. Both theories account for collective memories, knowledge, behavior, or images that we did not acquire in our personal lives; both account for transpersonal, collective, archetypal experience.

Through meditation or dreams, while in a mystical or ecstatic state, a person who taps into the collective unconscious or a morphic field has gained access to transpersonal experience where time and distance are immaterial. Sheldrake's analogy is that our DNA is like a television receiver that enables us to pick up transmissions; we "tune into" programs in the morphic field. Jung's collective unconscious has much the same implication: archetypal images, associated feelings, and patterns of behavior are the contents of the collective unconscious (or the field), of which we are unaware until they are activated and brought into consciousness. Plato was describing another variation on this same theme when he said that there exists a pure form to which everything like it is related, such as a perfect triangle. Aristotle described every entity as having a soul and said that the body is contained in the soul, rather than the soul in the body. The soul, then, would be a "field" that would influence and be influenced by the body. This idea has similarities to Sheldrake's theory that we resonate with the morphic field, influencing it and in turn being influenced by it.

That which we know gnostically may be knowledge received through tapping into a spiritual aspect of the morphic field. Taking the analogy of the television receiver further, the part of the psyche we are identified with or are in may determine the "channel" we tune into. The existence of an invisible "transmission" field suggests this possibility. If such is the case, then predictably, if we are in our soul or in touch with the Self (rather than identified with the ego or the persona or a complex), which is the inner attitude of the pilgrim, we will be open to receiving spiritual or soulful experiences.

Since morphic fields span time, they contain everything that has been important to human experience. History may forget, and there may be only faint traces of a matriarchal time when a Goddess was worshiped. But if morphic fields exist, images and rituals that have not been recalled for thousands of years will be accessible to people who turn again toward a goddess spirituality. If such is the case, then spontaneous rituals to the Goddess done by contemporary women are not invented but remembered. Tapping into a morphic field at a sacred site, a pilgrim may receive intuitively a truer sense of what went on there than would a scholar with limited sources from later though still relatively ancient times. Researchers dismiss the use of intuition, especially by women, as critics of archaeologist Marija Gimbutas have done because she made intuitive speculations about the meaning of shards and artifacts found at goddess sites. If morphic fields exist, and if she tapped into one, her conclusions would be correct.

There is a grassroots women's spirituality movement that is worldwide yet unorganized: women are gathering together in small groups or are acting individually, observing seasons and important transitions, doing rituals, making altars, finding symbols that express important spiritual and psychological themes and feelings. There is very little tradition to follow, and so women follow intuition and do what feels spontaneously right. After four to six thousand years of patriarchy and patriarchal gods, in the passing of spiritual traditions in a mother-line from mother to daughter, awareness of priestesses, healers, wisewomen, female divinity, or a Mother Goddess are lost from memory. In the spontaneous arising of a women's spirituality movement, however, "re-membering" may be occurring. In sacred places, where the Goddess once was worshiped or venerated, women enact rituals. In circles, women celebrate the seasons. Might it be that women are resonating with a morphic field as they bring the Goddess back into human consciousness? Might contemporary ritual reflect what has gone on before and be adding to it?

Experiences of the Goddess come through individuals who birth reemerging goddess consciousness through their own particular creative expression. While this is occurring mostly in women, it is not exclusively women through whom the Goddess is coming. She is appearing in the dreams of both men and women. The sacredness of the Earth and the body is felt by some men who also lack words for what they sense in their bodies as holy and are moved to express in some private act of reverence, ritual, or creativity.

SEVEN

Sister Pilgrims:
Glastonbury Tales

M rs. Detiger had arranged for Freya, an expert on Arthurian England, to be my companion on my journey to Glastonbury. In fact, throughout my journey, Mrs. Detiger made sure to include people as well as places on my itinerary. And as I went along, it became increasingly clear to me how important people were to the pilgrimage. Freya published a magazine that was an expression of her expertise and passion for Arthurian material and metaphor. The phone call from Mrs. Detiger inviting Freya "to accompany Jean Bolen on a pilgrimage" came to her on the same day that my book *Goddesses in Every-woman* finally reached her bedstand. It had been in a "to read" stack of books for well over six months, and on that very day she had finally started to read it. She had the edition with my photograph as the back cover; it was on the table next to the phone when it rang.

There was an additional significance to the timing of the invitation. Had it come any earlier, she would have declined, for her strength had just begun to return after many months of convalescence. She had had a hysterectomy and radiation for cancer that had spread from the cervix to invade the lymphatic system. And, like me, in the previous year she had separated from her husband. Thus the invitation came to her, as it did to me, at a crucial juncture in her life, and synchronicity was playing a part in making her a Sister Pilgrim.

I know that synchronistic events and meetings are like waking dreams, full of symbols and themes that one should heed. Thus I wondered about the significance of her name, Freya. Freya was the name of the Great Goddess of northern Europe, the goddess of fertility, love, the moon, the sea, the earth, the underworld, death, birth, virgin, mother, ancestress. She had so many attributes that scholars who tried to affix one label to her could not. In sum, she was as many-sided as any other version of the Great Goddess.

Freya was the goddess of youth, love, and beauty in Richard Wagner's *The Ring of the Nibelung,* whom Wotan agreed to give to the giants in payment for building Valhalla, his fortress-castle and monument to his everlasting fame and manhood. This is a repeated theme in patriarchal mythology: it is Agamemnon in *The Iliad,* sacrificing his daughter Iphigenia in order that his army could sail to Troy; it is Zeus agreeing that Hades could abduct Persephone. It is also the metaphor for the psychology of men who trade their youth, the importance of love, and an appreciation for beauty to their ambition. They sacrifice their *anima,* suppressing the feminine aspect of their psyches for power. The feminine is not allowed to develop and contribute to the creativity, sensitivity, and perspective of the male personality. The anima—symbolized by the maiden—is seen and treated in much the same way as women, devalued and suppressed to the same degree.

This happens in women, as well. Disowning youthful Freya qualities is the price of success in a man's world. A woman cannot succeed if she is perceived as being too feminine, tenderhearted, vulnerable, or emotional. Nor can she usually succeed if she has the confidence in herself of the Great Goddess Freya, for she then does not know her place.

While Freya's name brought these goddesses to mind, it was an actual woman who would be joining me on this pilgrimage, and who she was could turn out to be very significant. Like the pilgrims in *The Canterbury Tales,* or the fellow travelers in Katherine Anne Porter's *Ship of Fools*, whose own personal stories we come to know, our fellow or sister travelers on any significant journey are individuals whose stories we learn about and take to heart. Our companions are often important symbolically as well. They can represent inner figures, aspects of significant others in our lives, possibilities for what we might ourselves become, reminders of who we were, or metaphors for our life situation. Who, I wondered, would Freya turn out to be?

Pilgrim's Progress: Glastonbury Tales

Over a five-hour dinner, Freya told me her story, and I told her mine. I found that she had been given a 50/50 prognosis, and in that first conversation, it was clear to both of us that this pilgrimage might make the difference between her living and dying. Conversational depth came easily. I learned that in the year before we met, she had gone through extensive major surgery and the highest advisable dose of radiation to combat what otherwise would be and still could be a terminal disease. I know how overwhelming and benumbing the onslaught of disease, diagnostic procedures, and treatment usually are, and of the enormous toll they take on all resources, which I learned later had not only been physically and emotionally depleting but had left her financially impoverished as well. In addition, she told me that one of her dearest friends had died unexpectedly during this same harrowing time that she separated from her husband and had to give up a dream job.

Now physically well enough to travel, she tired easily and was aware—as I was also on this pilgrimage—of being in a mythic time and in a mythic landscape that had personal meaning for each of us. She was at the most vulnerable time in her life both psychologically and physically. She was indeed at a life-and-death crossroad: this pilgrimage would determine the direction that her body and her spirit would take.

At this moment Freya reminded me of Psyche in the story of *Eros and Psyche*. Psyche was a mythological heroine whose path many women find themselves following, when they are on their own and their survival depends upon being able to do more than they think possible.

Like most women, Psyche appeared to be an unheroic figure. Abandoned, rejected, and pregnant, alone and overwhelmed, she wanted to die and tried to drown herself in the river. The river itself threw her back on the riverbank, as an instinctive life force in women often does. Unable to not go on, she was then confronted with the necessity of accomplishing a series of initially impossible tasks. Each time, a part of her despaired—it was too hard, she wanted to give up—while at the same time, she stayed with the task. Then, as also happens in life, help came and enabled her to succeed. In the myth, the helpers are symbolic. In life, while real people are important, a woman taps into sources within herself and finds that courage, intuition, intelligence, and previously undeveloped abilities come forth and make it possible to do what it is she has to do.

During significant junctures and passages when the former fabric of life comes apart at the seams and old patterns unravel, dreams and synchronicities often become more important and numerous. It is a time to pay attention to the people we encounter and events that occur as being both real and symbolic. Besides just being herself, Freya could then symbolize a possibility in me, as I might represent something in her. I especially wondered about this because of an unusual conversation that I had had the day I met Freya, just before leaving the Netherlands. Mrs. Detiger had left me a message saying "an interesting wise old woman would like to speak to you. She is the Sensitive of the Dutch Royal Family and is expected to die quite soon. She noticed your aura and has made a special point of following your experience while in Europe." I did not have time to see her in person, so I called. She invited me to ask her questions, which I did. I was impressed with the comments and answers she provided to my inquiries, and so I took it in when she cautioned me about my health, which as far as I knew was excellent, warning me that something serious could develop. She would not or could not be any more specific than this.

Freya and I were in major periods of personal transition since we each had separated from our husbands. We told each other about our marriages, the circumstances that led to the decision to leave, and the decision's impact on others. Both of us had children whose welfare we were concerned about. My daughter and son were both in their early teens; her two sons were years younger. I later became aware that this was also the time when we both crossed into menopause, shifting physiologically from mother to wisewoman-crone. Freya had had a hysterectomy and had consequently entered a surgically induced menopause at forty and, unknowable to me at the time, I was having my last menstrual period at Glastonbury; the month I returned home from the pilgrimage I turned fifty.

I had left a basically good man and a marriage that had dysfunctional parts but had a lot of good going for it. We had been good partners pulling in the traces together, putting together a household, being parents, and supporting each other's work in the world. We didn't address emotionally charged issues and when a crunch came, we couldn't. Our communication was fine about the logistics of life, but inadequate to the needs of emotional intimacy or real friendship. We couldn't express our vulnerabilities, needs, anger, disappointments.

This was in marked contrast to what occurred elsewhere. In my psychiatric work, the fifty-minute hours are filled with intensity, search, emotions, and depth; here I can reflect back what I am hearing by tapping into my own depths as well as being affected by the encounter. Maintaining rapport while in the midst of whatever comes up in the session is a practice much like meditation. Working through differences is not only possible but also deepens the therapeutic relationship; in the process of doing depth work, the analyst is affected. This is the alchemy of Jungian analysis: if the patient is to be affected by the process, so also must the doctor. While Jungian analysis is a genuine dialogue, the contents and the focus are the patient's material. A hunger for a two-way dialogue kept growing in me and I kept growing more lonely in my marriage, a situation that I thought might not have arisen had I been in some other occupation.

However, I hear of this same loneliness and hunger for depth communication from women in other circumstances and know how common it is to feel this way. The need to share what we experience, to be listened to, to have what is going on *inside* of us matter to the person we are married to, to engage in a two-way dialogue, is the cry of one soul yearning to meet another.

Maybe the end of my marriage and the circumstances that led to its dissolution also had something to do with the transit of the planet Uranus, which governs transformations and abrupt changes. I had gotten my first serious astrological reading shortly after I left my husband and home, not expecting that it could be so precise in its to-the-month timing of significant preceding events, which gave it credibility and provided me with some bearings. In the unfamiliar language of astrology, this Uranus impacted a Grand Cross to shake up four areas of my life—personality, work, children, and marriage—a configuration that comes around every forty-nine years. From the perspective of the astrological chart, it was a time of crisis that would break me if I were to be caught between the opposites; I could be crucified on the Grand Cross unless I grew "large enough" to contain these opposites within my psyche and my life. According to this reading, Uranus would not appear again in this configuration until my ninety-eighth year, if I should live that long. This would be the time to make that last transformation from life to death. The gravity and significance of death felt to me an apt comparison to what was happening. On a symbolic level, I had died to my old life and was no longer who I had been.

While there are exceptions, men and women both turn to women to be seen and understood. I had developed a deep soul connection with a woman that had created a crisis in my marriage and led to this separation. It had begun as a need in my psyche for communication and depth and ended up taking me into the spiritual dimension of the feminine. The woman was a disruptive catalyst for change, and her presence in my life was not something that my husband and I were able to survive as a couple. A dialogue was simply not possible. We became polarized strangers and reached an impasse.

Communication between my husband and me had become painfully blocked, and I left benumbed, feeling emotionally battered and in a state of conflict and confusion. I knew that he was hurting and that he felt a profound sense of betrayal and some self-blame, but I felt emotionally battered by his anger and interrogation and had become increasingly mute and numb. Neither of us were the people we used to be with each other. Meanwhile, appalled at what our relationship was doing to my marriage and convinced that I would abandon her, my woman friend withdrew from me and went into Zen meditation as the first of many steps that, by degrees, would take her out of my life.

Bearing Witness to One Another's Lives

I am convinced of the importance of having a significant person bear witness to our lives. I often think that this is what I do as a psychiatrist: I witness my patients' lives and thus know what it is like in their particular circumstances and what it means to be them. They share with me those moments and relationships that truly matter. I know of the courage and sacrifices, of the guilt and shame that couldn't be forgiven or faced until whatever it was could be told. And years later, when someone comes back to let me know what has happened to them in intervening years, I can again bear witness, as I listen and know the significance of what they tell me.

We all share a need to be totally honest, to be able to speak to another human being who accepts us as we are, and believes in us, about what we have done and what was done to us, about what we hope for, think about, fear, and feel. This can be, of course, the province of friends as well as therapists, if our friends are people with whom we can speak openly, knowing that whatever we say in confidence will not be repeated to others, will not be held against us or used against us. All too often, unfortunately, we hold back the full truth because expectations and assumptions about what we should feel or think and how we should act get in the way.

It is no small matter to be a witness to another person's life story. By listening with compassion, we validate each other's lives, make suffering meaningful, and help the process of forgiving and healing to take place. And our acceptance may make it possible for a person who feels outside the human community to gain a sense of belonging once more. Men who returned from Vietnam needed such witnesses. Those who were able to become part of the community again (unlike the veterans who in their isolation, guilt, and rage are still, psychologically, among the missing) were able to do so because they told their stories, often over and over again, to other human beings who, by listening compassionately, accepted them back into the ordinary world.

Survivors of childhood abuse are in a similar situation. They also feel ashamed, defective, or different, "beyond the pale," because of what they experienced. They, too, need to tell what happened to them, to have someone bear witness to their lives in order to feel that they belong.

Any significant, soul-shaping event becomes more integrated into our consciousness, and more universal, when we can express the essence of the experience and have it received in depth by another. I am convinced that any human being who can serve as witness for another at a soul level heals the separateness and isolation that we might otherwise feel. Witnessing is not a one-way experience; the witness is also affected by the encounter. To comprehend the truth of another person's experience, we must truly take it in and be affected.

Ritual Time

When Freya and I had a soul-to-soul conversation over dinner, each of us bore witness to the other's life at a crucial time. In doing so, we became sister pilgrims who, like pilgrims in days of old, told how we had come to be on this pilgrimage and the circumstances of our lives. There was, however, another even deeper significance to this conversation that also had to do with witnessing. Witnessing is—in a ritual sense—the hearing of each other's confession, which is the opening movement in the archetypal symphony of redemption and healing. This is where all such spiritual rituals and most therapies begin. The first step in any healing process is to tell what happened, to someone who listens without judgment.

This conversation took place the evening before our last morning in Glastonbury. On that last morning, we were invited to participate in a ritual. Had it not been for our witnessing, the ritual would not have had the power that it had for me.

Freya and I were up at 6:00 A.M. to meet Ann Jevons, the woman who would lead the ritual. We waited in the high-ceilinged front room of our bed and breakfast for forty-five minutes, at which point we decided we'd better go next door and find her. We threw a couple of pebbles at an upstairs window and were rewarded when a cheerful Ann popped her head out the window and saw us. She hadn't expected us to be up and about this early. In a pastel jogging suit, her usual morning garb, Ann appeared to be a most unlikely priestess. She's a friendly, outgoing, energetic person, with the outer facade of an extroverted flight attendant, which she once was. She and her husband, David, a former commercial pilot, run Chalice Hill House, the bed-and-breakfast inn where we were staying. When they had moved to Glastonbury, Ann had had a vision that had inspired the ritual that we were about to experience. We would go to the Garden of the Chalice Well and then onto the grounds of the ruins of Glastonbury Abbey, both of which were close by. At this early morning hour, there would be no other people there.

The Chalice Well

In Glastonbury legend, the Chalice Well in Glastonbury and the Sacred Well of Avalon are considered one and the same. The well is a natural spring that lies between Glastonbury Tor and Chalice Hill. It rises inside a stone well shaft nine feet deep and flows abundantly, some twenty-five thousand gallons a day. The water contains iron, and though it appears crystal clear, the shallow watercourse and pools through which it flows are stained blood red by the iron. It was once called Blood Spring or Blood Well.

Once more, the name Chalice Well and the iron-tinged water suggest a sacred vessel filled with blood, this time rising out of Mother Earth at the site that "was Avalon."

The well is in a serene and beautiful garden, and at this time of year apple trees were in blossom, a profusion of flowers were in bloom, vines and climbing roses grew over walls, and the grass was thick and green. Winding paths take the visitor upward, through portals between terraced levels and past sheltering trees, inviting benches, and peaceful vistas. There is a feel of Avalon about the place, even though the garden is just off a well-traveled road.

Sacred wells fed by underground springs were often found at goddess sites. The well might later be ignored once the site became Christian—as at Chartres Cathedral, where the well is in the crypt, its lid locked. Or a well that was once sacred to the Goddess might have been renamed and reconsecrated to a female saint; in Ireland, such wells became "Brigid wells" after Saint Brigid. In mythology and legend, Goddesses and springs are often found together. In Norse mythology as in Richard Wagner's opera cycle *The Ring of the Nibelung,* for instance, the Goddess (Erda) was a source of wisdom, and drinking from the spring was a means of tapping into this source.

The water of the Chalice Well is cold and delicious, and shared with anyone who wants to drink it or fill a container. Water flows out of a font in a low garden terrace wall below the well, where it is readily accessible, and then descends to enter a large shallow pool in the shape of overlapping circles, the design of the *vesica piscis,* at the lower end of the garden.

The Chalice Well garden has a wall around it and is entered through a gate. However, even when the garden is not open to visitors, a perpetual flow of water comes through an outlet to the side street, where people can fill their containers and drink at any time.

Dion Fortune, a psychologist with a strong interest in the occult, wrote of the Chalice Well in *Avalon of the Heart* and said that there is a large chamber that opens out of the well shaft, with a recess large enough for a person to stand in or the Grail to be hidden, and that on the summer solstice, a shaft of light shines straight into this inner chamber. The chamber is made of great blocks of stone such as were used at Stonehenge, stone that cannot be found in the immediate area. The masonry is perfectly true and square, brought there and constructed by means we cannot imagine.

In 1919, the well was given a lid, which was decorated with a wrought-iron design called the *vesica piscis* by Frederick Bligh Bond. Bligh Bond authored *The Gate of Remembrance*, the book I had looked for after dreaming of the knight in the room under the cathedral. I finally found the book in a Glastonbury bookshop.

Bligh Bond was a respected scholar who was appointed director of excavations at Glastonbury Abbey in 1909. His curious little book recounts the successful excavations of the foundation of the Chapel of Loretto, the Edgar Chapel, and other buildings on the abbey grounds. Information about where to dig had come through automatic writing, a form of mediumship in which a person in a trance writes messages purported to be from people who have died. The accurate locations and dimensions of these ruins were described in Latin; the informants claimed to have lived in the sixteenth century when the abbey had flourished. They identified themselves as "William the Monk" and "Johannes the Stonemason." Johannes said he had died in 1533. The use of psychic means, however successful, tarnished Bligh Bond's reputation and cost him his position. There are many things about Glastonbury that have an air of otherworldliness about them.

The Vesica Piscis

I was still wearing the *vesica piscis* pendant that had come in Mrs. Detiger's letter of invitation. It was beautiful. I had put it on immediately and worn it ever since, which made it a very familiar shape.

Vesica piscis means "vessel of the fish" in Latin. The basic design is made by overlapping the edges of two circles of equal size, the circumference of each of which passes through the center of the other, which creates an almond shape (a mandorla) or pointed oval between them.

When the two circles are one above the other, the shape between them becomes an outline of the body of a fish, which was a symbol of Christ, an easily drawn symbol that early Christians used to identify themselves to one another. It is said that the reason for using the fish as a Christian symbol was that the Greek word for fish, *ichthys*, can

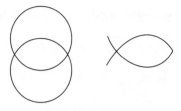

be an acronym for Jesus Christ, Son of God. However, before it became a Christian symbol, the *vesica piscis* was a universal symbol of the Mother Goddess, the almond shaped mandorla representing an outline of her vulva, through which all life came. According to Barbara Walker in *The Woman's Encyclopedia of Myths and Secrets*, this was unequivocally so.

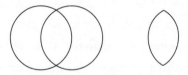

To be a symbol of the Goddess, the circles overlap side to side and the almond shape has its pointed ends up and down. As for the name *vesica piscis,* the vulva is said to have a slightly fishy smell; in Greek, the word *delphos* means both womb and fish; and there are many cross-cultural associations between goddess and fish. The temple door images of the Hindu goddess Kali and the female figure Sheila-na-gig, which was carved or sculptured in the entry arch of old Irish churches, display their vulvas as vesicas. Many Catholic medallions are in this shape as well.

The *vesica piscis* on the lid of the Chalice Well and on the pendant I wear incorporates the overlapping circles, one above the other, but in a more complex design. The two circles are contained within a larger circle or round. On both sides of this basic *vesica piscis* are vine and leaf patterns, and in the center is a vertical rod that seems to grow out of or go into plant life at the base.

Without making any analysis, I was drawn to the beauty of the pendant, which is how it is with symbols; we are attracted to (or repelled by) objects that have some kind of charge on them for us; this makes them symbolic objects and not just things. Usually they constellate something in us or receive an unconscious projection. Then, as is the case for me, one's mind becomes engaged, wondering, What is it about this that touches me personally?

I came to think of the *vesica piscis,* the image of two overlapping spheres, as a visual metaphor for those moments when worlds overlap or interpenetrate and life is imbued with depth and meaning. These are for me "*vesica piscis* experiences"; intersections of the timeless with time. Here occur those moments in and out of time when the visible world and the invisible world intersect; when eternal values and the mundane world overlap; when the archetypal world and the tangible world meet; when Heaven and Earth, the upper world and the lower one, come together in a liminal moment. When we, for example, know what T. S. Eliot means when he writes of "music heard so deeply / that it is not heard at all, but you are the music / while the music lasts." When we can know that which is deeply meaningful and beyond what we can grasp intellectually. When we can have mystical or poetic insight.

How appropriate then that this image be connected with Glastonbury, where, in literary imagination and legend, one could cross through the mists to Avalon and drink from the sacred well.

Ritual at the Well

Ann led us inside the walls of the Garden of the Chalice Well, which I was seeing for the first time. We walked past two overlapping shallow pools shaped like a *vesica piscis* that over time had turned in color from white to blood red. Then we followed the path that led us under arches and up through terraced areas to the place where water flows out of a font. And there, she took us through a purification ritual, using the Chalice Well water throughout. How could there be a more beautiful or powerful place to do such a thing?

With words and gestures, we were enacting a ritual of cleansing, purifying, and letting go—of negativity, of fear, of the past, of people, of expectations, of whatever stood in the way of our openness and receptivity to divinity, to love, healing, hope, vision, wisdom, whatever. We let the clear water from the font wash over our hands and arms, and then, cupping our hands, we filled them, washed our faces, and drank deeply. In prayer and meditation, we thought of what we specifically needed to let go of as we filled our cupped hands with water, and in throwing the water away and shaking the last drops off our hands, we ritualized our intentions and invoked help that we might be able to do what we needed to do to let go of emotional burdens and bonds, in order to heal our souls.

The Abbey

The next part of our ritual took us to the ruins of Glastonbury Abbey. Retracing our steps, we now headed back toward the town of Glastonbury.

Glastonbury Abbey has been called "the holyest erthe in Englande," where once stood a Celtic monastery, the first Christian community in the British Isles, and later the most important church in England. What remains now are the abbey's graceful ruins. Some of the arches of the nave still stand, outlined against the sky, as do some of the outlying buildings. The acres of abbey grounds are carpeted with soft deep-green grass. A rectangular area outlined by a chain shows where the High Altar once stood.

Another marker notes where the bones claimed to be those of Arthur and Guinevere were once interred. There are pathways and walks. The roofless Lady Chapel built over the site of the first church in Christendom to be dedicated to Mary is the most intact building.

We entered the abbey grounds from the back of the property, walking between two huge oaks, and came to where the nave had been. It was still early, and again we were the only people here. Ann had led the way, and now she asked us to take off our shoes so that we could stand barefooted on the High Altar. With an attitude of reverence, Freya and I stepped onto the grassy rectangular site where the High Altar once had been. Ann told us that two ley lines crossed at the High Altar, making this the power point of the abbey.

Rituals take place within sacred time and space. That is certainly what it felt like, as I stood with my bare feet on a rectangle of Mother Earth that was simultaneously the High Altar. Ann, as her priestess self, was now fully present, jogging suit and all.

I entered a deeply receptive state of consciousness, so I cannot say exactly what she said, though I can say something about what went on within me. I once again felt my Christian spirituality: Christ, Holy Spirit, God the Father were with me once more. And I felt the presence of a Mother God, the Goddess, as well. Standing on the High Altar, listening to a contemporary priestess, I could feel energy from Mother Earth coming up through my feet into my body, while the Spirit descended from above through my head. Both came together and met in my heart. It felt as if a large chalice, glowing with light, filled my entire chest.

This coming together of God and Goddess healed a split in me. Though I had for a long time begun my prayers with "Dear Mother-Father God," before this I'd not felt the two energies come together in me. If anything, the two aspects of the Deity seemed to be getting further and further apart for me, as I experienced the sacredness of feminine divinity and grew increasingly informed and angry at what had happened to the Goddess historically and the consequence of this for women. God had become equated in my mind with oppressive patriarchal power, with the Inquisition and the burning times, with narrow-minded fundamentalists who were full of fear and hatred, with the jealous and vengeful god of the Old Testament. I had become distant, cut off from my own momentous experience of God's grace and loving presence. On the High Altar, when God and Goddess ineffably came together in me, I was reunited with the loving God that I had "known."

Ann's voice receded and then she was silent. My eyes closed and I had no sense of time. Now a ritual of my own seemed to suggest itself. One at a time, I sensed the most important people in my life. I mentally spoke with each one, and thanked them for what they had done for me, or been for me, or taught me. I asked them to forgive me for the pain I had caused them. And I forgave them and freed them of my expectations. In this ritual, I saw the people in my life in a loving light, consciously willed that I could forgive and let go of feelings that bound me to pain or guilt.

I believe that emotional patterns are affected by rituals. In much the same way that children building sand castles at the edge of the sea dig channels in the sand and affect where the water will flow, so do rituals, intentions, prayers, and meditations provide invisible channels for emotions that surge up. Sometimes an unexpectedly large wave of emotion floods all our efforts, however. And if the tide of emotion is coming in, rather than going out, then it is not the time to do what I was doing at Glastonbury Abbey. For feelings of grief and anger must be allowed to wash through us and over us before we can work on those channels that allow us to forgive and let go.

The opportunity to let go and forgive presents itself over and over again in times of transition, when it is no longer possible to hold on to what was or might have been. This is when waves of positive and negative feelings, memories, longings, blame and self-blame, dreams, regrets, reminders of past experience and once-held hopes come surging up.

When I remember standing on the grass that was the site of the High Altar in Glastonbury Abbey, I realize I was enacting the *vesica piscis* in myself. The two spheres, Christian and Goddess, Father and Mother God, archetypal and ordinary, intersected in me. As I stood there, I was in that moment "the rod" that connected the two worlds as well. Surrounded by the greenness of the setting, I was the recipient of grace, which made me feel whole. This all came together in my heart, in a profound inner spiritual sacramental moment.

EIGHT

Avalon: Otherworld and Motherworld

I n *The Mists of Avalon,*
Avalon is the island home of the Priestesses of the Goddess. It is hidden from the Glastonbury of the monks, behind the mists, accessible only to those who can call the
barge. Psychologically, Avalon is an archetypal otherworld
and a mother realm. There is something about the Glastonbury Tor that evokes the image of the otherworld even
today. I think it has something to do with its prominence

and unnatural terraced shape, its soft greenness, the quality of light, and especially the power or energy that people feel there.

Avalon, like the mythological Shambala, the fictional Mount Analogue, and the legendary Grail Castle, is an otherworld place, visible only under special conditions and to particular people. In the British Isles, the otherworld across the water has been called "the Green Isle in the West," "the Land beyond the Sea," and "the Island of Women." In Ireland, the otherworld is imagined to lie buried under mounds or hills; its inhabitants (like Avalon's) are the people of the Goddess, the *Tuatha Dé Danann*.

At Chalice Hill House, the bed-and-breakfast inn that was home for the duration of my stay in Glastonbury, I saw a photograph of the Tor and the hilly area adjacent to it taken in the last decade at a time of flooding, when much of the area around Glastonbury was under water. It was a picture of an island. The photograph was a reminder of the connection between Glastonbury and the Isle of Avalon, and *Ynys-witrin,* its Celtic name, which means "the Isle of Glass."

Glastonbury and other sacred sites are places where the ordinary world and the otherworld seemingly overlap and more readily evoke psychic or spiritual impressions. Besides its association with Avalon, Glastonbury Tor was also regarded centuries ago as a point of entry to Annwn, the Celtic otherworld. They are landscapes that affect us like dreams or poems or music, that move us out of our everyday reality into a deeper archetypal realm; where images and feelings, intuitions or sensations that we otherwise would not feel are felt. Myth and legend that touch the same psychological depths have a similar evocative effect on the imagination and mood. We leave the ordinary world behind and venture into another world.

We can be affected by a story as much as we can be by a dream, if its symbols and events have a certain mystery and power for us that in turn evoke our own memories and thoughts. We can be struck by the story's message, or have a flash of insight that illuminates something we had not seen before, much in the same way that a major dream affects us. When a story holds meaning for a people and a time as did the Grail legend, it becomes a myth for the age; and unless and until there is an official version, there will be embellishments, deletions, and additions, for the story is a living vehicle for the psyche of the teller and the listener. In choosing which of the versions to use, what to emphasize and muse about, I am following that tradition of bards, poets, and storytellers who have told and retold the Grail story over the centuries. As Joseph Campbell said of this tradition: "You take a traditional story and interpret it—give it new depth and meaning in terms of the conditions of your particular day."

Nowhere is the impact of retelling Arthurian legend clearer than in Marion Zimmer Bradley's *The Mists of Avalon,* where new depth and meaning is given to the familiar story of King Arthur and the Knights of the Round Table by looking at the story from the perspective of the women. The story begins before Arthur is conceived and ends soon after his death. The era is presented as a time of religious transition, during which Christianity gains ascendancy over the Goddess and Avalon disappears into the mists. It is through the eyes and conflicted heart of Arthur's half-sister Morgaine, the last priestess of the Goddess, that we follow the unfolding events. It is a familiar story told from an entirely unfamiliar perspective. Bradley, a prolific writer of fantasy and science fiction, writes knowingly, as if she *is* Morgaine.

The book strikes a chord in many women. We feel as if we are hearing something about our past about which we have no memory, and then when we are reminded, we feel in our bones that it is true. It is like hearing a missing part of our own history. As for Avalon, it is an archetypal place, psychologically, that touches anyone who yearns to come home to the Goddess and so can imagine responding as Morgaine herself does on seeing Avalon:

> Then, like a curtain being pulled back, the mist vanished, and before them lay a sunlit stretch of water and a green shore. . . . The light—could it be the same sun she knew?—flooded the land with gold and silence, and she felt her throat tighten with tears. She thought, without knowing why, "I am coming home."

This story rings true because its essential narrative did take place in human history—probably not in Arthurian Britain but certainly in Old Europe, where for thousands of years before the invasion by Indo-European warrior people there existed a Goddess culture of agricultural people and artisans who valued fertility and peace and were attuned to the seasons and to the earth. These "mother cultures" that preceded patriarchy have been well described by Marija Gimbutas, Merlin Stone, and Riane Eisler. Somewhere in us, we know of a time when this feminine principle prevailed, a time of the Goddess, of the sacredness of sexuality and fertility, of our link to the earth. Somehow we know that there once were priestesses, healers, and wisewomen who were keepers of knowledge.

For women to respond this deeply to fiction suggests that it corresponds with some growing edge in us. For most of us, after all, the whole notion of "goddess" and "priestess" is foreign to the religious traditions in which we were raised. Even in fiction, this notion would be difficult to relate to unless a change in consciousness were occurring. Clothed in Arthurian personae, the characters in *The Mists of Avalon* put us in touch with a myth that reflects an aspect of human history that is relevant now, because we are entering another time of transition when once again the values of the patriarchy interact and clash with those of a returning goddess consciousness and an awareness that the Goddess and woman—in moments out of ordinary time—are one and the same. In moments in which a human woman "is the Goddess" or the Great Mother, she makes the moment sacred, shares her body and confers a blessing through it.

Morgaine assumes this role when she is holding a dying Arthur and they are crossing the water to Avalon in the barge. She says, "And so Arthur lay at last with his head in my lap, seeing in me neither sister nor lover, nor foe, but only wise-woman, priestess, Lady of the Lake; and so rested upon the breast of the Great Mother from whom he came to birth and to whom at last, as all men, he must go."

Morgaine is helping Arthur to make the crossing from life to death. When he is dying, she is the Comforter, there to hold him, so that he need not feel fearful and alone. He is, at that moment, in the arms of the Goddess, whom he experiences through the warmth and touch and love of a human woman. Thus she is a priestess through whom the divinity of the Goddess, the Great Mother, comes. It becomes a sacramental moment; through her, his last moments can be infused with peace, safety, and grace. Morgaine is functioning as a midwife, easing a soul over the threshold at death, as she and others might also midwife life at the moment of birth. These transition times once were the province of women and are part of the mysteries that are being reclaimed.

Women as Midwives of the Soul

I have spoken with women who have instinctively held a dying person in their arms. When I called them midwives of the soul at the transition time of death, each woman recognized this as being exactly what she felt. I am convinced that women need to tell others of this experience, so that none of us will be inhibited by the fear that we're being inappropriate and stifle the urge.

Three weeks before my friend Valerie flew east to be at her dying mother's hospital bedside, I told her about attending the memorial service for our friend Isabel's adult daughter. There I heard Isabel speak of getting in bed with her comatose daughter and holding her in her arms for hours until she died, and of the profound peacefulness that she experienced throughout the night and at the moment of death. Valerie remembered Isabel's story the evening she visited her mother at the hospital, and knew the instant she walked into the room—from the change in her mother's breathing—that her mother was dying. Wanting to help her leave, as her mother had helped her come into the world, Valerie got into her mother's hospital bed and held her, feeling her mother's body respond to being held; thus comforted, her mother died.

Two years before in Costa Rica, Therese, another woman who now works with the dying, told me a similar story of getting into a hospital bed with a man who she could only hold easily by sitting behind him. Embracing him from behind she began to breathe with him; as his breathing became slower and deeper, she could feel his fear leave, and he died peacefully. These are sacramental experiences, where a woman functions as priestess, Comforter, Mother Goddess, and herself shares a holy moment through her body.

Women as Vessels of the Goddess

That the body of a woman can be a vessel through which the Goddess comes is an unexpected revelation, a revelation that does not come through illumination, vision, or insight, which is how masculine divinity manifests, but through an embodied experience—through intimate, caring, reverent touch that is simultaneously sensual and sacred, deeply personal and transpersonal. This is a secret that is kept from women, who as a gender learn to dislike the roundness and fullness of their bodies, feel ashamed about the blood mysteries of menarche, menstruation, and menopause, want to be put to sleep when they give birth, and are horrified on awakening from dreams in which they lovingly embraced a woman.

Many women who are initiated into their own bodies by the Goddess have explored the body of the Goddess in another woman, either a real woman or in vivid dreams; these experiences can deeply affirm being a woman and being in the body of a woman. They also can confuse and terrify women. Another woman's body mirrors her own, boundaries between them dissolve, and a merging that encompasses the totality of both bodies and auras can occur that may recollect dim sensory memories of mother and infant merger or be the first time this archetype is experienced. The experience with another woman may allow a woman to become an actively sensual person where before she had been passive or reactive in her responses. Whether in dreams (where the symbolic meaning also needs exploring) or lived out, embodiment as a sexual and sensual woman results if she embraces the lover aspect of herself; the opposite occurs if she becomes terrified that she is a sinful, perverted person and must suppress her sensuality.

Confusion about sexual orientation occurs; it is and yet it isn't about sexual orientation at all. It is an invocation and integration of the sensual aspects of the Demeter, Persephone, Hera, or Aphrodite archetype in the woman that now may become consciously present in the sexual relationships she enters; whether with a man or a woman, she now may become embodied and sensual. That it isn't necessarily about sexual orientation is what has been confusing, especially for women who, having been exclusively heterosexual, fall in love with a woman or with the Goddess in a woman, decide they are lesbians, and then later fall in love with a man.

A deep sense of *union* can occur when a man and woman make love; in the physical fit, in the coming together of the two sexes, a completion and wholeness can be experienced; it can also be a sacramental experience and a holy encounter. When lovemaking at a similar soul level takes place between two women, the experience is a *reunion* rather than union. While the opportunity and capacity to have either or both experiences is an individual matter, they are part of women's archetypal potential. This physical and mystical encounter with another through a meeting of both soul and body brings both individuals into the realm of Mystery; *communion* can then take place.

When there was awe and reverence for Aphrodite, before she and her sexuality were desecrated, a man who came to her temple to ritually enter a physical communion would have approached the woman who was to be the embodiment of the Goddess hoping or knowing that through her he might experience the Goddess. She would be his priestess, not a prostitute—a holy woman, not a fallen woman. In Celtic tradition, as fictionalized in *The Mists of Avalon*, Morgaine was the Goddess when she lay with Arthur, who had proven himself worthy of enacting the ritual union in which a man became the Horned God and king.

In fundamental patriarchy, a woman's sexuality and ability to bear children belongs exclusively to her husband and not to the woman herself. The sexual and sensual realms are feared and repressed. In the collective memory of women, we know that death by stoning, as well as rape and impoverishment and forced prostitution were the penalties for unsanctioned sexuality. Thus terror often accompanies forbidden sexual feelings, recollecting that the power of God and man was brought to bear against the Goddess and the autonomy of women.

Avalon as an Archetypal Motherworld

Avalon is psychologically a motherworld. It is in the shadow of patriarchal consciousness, repressed and thus feared and distorted, as are any contents of the personal or collective unconscious that are denied. It is also the world of the Mother we once lived in if we were cherished in infancy; in growing up, we left this behind. This motherworld is personally prehistoric, before our own specific memories, as matriarchal history is also. Avalon as motherworld also continues to exist, side by side with rational consciousness, to be entered only when we alter consciousness by falling asleep and dreaming, fall in love, or are in a situation in which the veils between the worlds are thinner and we cross over.

Our sense of time alters when we cross into Avalon. The Greeks had two words for time, *kairos* and *kronos*. Time as we know it in the rational world is linear and measured *kronos*, which we keep track of by clocks or chronometers, dervied from *Kronos*, the name of the Greek god who swallowed his children. Time in the fatherworld enters each January 1 symbolized by an infant and departs on December 31 as Father Time, a long-bearded, bent-over old man. In the motherworld, we participate in time and thus lose track of it; the Greek word for this quality of time is *kairos*. Whenever we are doing something that we love and are totally absorbed in the doing of it, we are in kairos rather than *kronos* time, whenever we are with someone we love and totally absorbed in being with that person, whenever we are in love, whenever what we are doing nourishes the soul, we are out of ordinary time and in the motherworld.

When Glastonbury and Avalon were said to once coexist, it was possible to cross over only if one could call the barge and cross through the mists. The Queendom of the Goddess was at hand, but not all had access to it. This notion is a variation of mystical traditions in which alternate realities exist for the initiate to enter. For the Christian mystic, it is the Kingdom of God.

A model for the existence of motherworld and father-world exists as right and left brain psychology, in which the dominant left brain is rational, verbal, and linear, while the right brain is nonverbal, nonrational, nonlinear. The function of the right brain is less appreciated but has to do with images, emotional coloration of experiences, and song (if words at all); the right brain is open to alternative realities.

Remembering Mother

To cross to Avalon is to remember the archetypal Mother, the Goddess in her several forms and many names, to rediscover the feminine mysteries and the sacred in embodied experiences. Avalon exists where divinity dwells in nature and quickens it in the pilgrim. Where there is feminine divinity, there is access to Avalon. But once patriarchal religion and male gods prevailed, Avalon, the Grail, and the Goddess all disappeared into the mists of forgotten time. It is as if Avalon moved farther and farther away from humankind—at least that part that calls itself Western civilization. The Grail also disappeared from the world, and inasmuch as a sacred chalice is a symbol of the Goddess, no wonder it, too, left a world that no longer remembered Mother and only acknowledged Father.

The Grail legend struck several chords that are thematic reminders that something of great value was lost from ordinary reality. The mysterious Grail still exists but does so in an otherworld location. It is in the Grail Castle carried by the Grail maiden. It is in a place that Perceval, the innocent fool, stumbled into, only to have the place disappear when he failed to adequately appreciate the experience. And, significantly, Perceval found the Grail Castle only after he remembered his mother and set off to find her.

At the beginning of the Grail story, we meet Perceval as a youth who has been raised in the forest. Thus when he sees knights in armor on horseback for the first time, he doesn't know what they are. He is awed and says to them, "You must be angels!" revealing himself to be an innocent or a fool. Told by his mother that the most beautiful beings he could ever hope to see are angels, he mistakenly assumes that this is what they are. When they tell him that they are knights, Perceval immediately seeks to become one himself and leaves his mother without so much as a backward glance. Perceval is successful at this calling. He challenges knights, wins armor, finds a mentor, and is knighted. It is only after all of this that Perceval suddenly remembers his mother and sets out to find her, which is the quest he is on when he meets the Fisher King and comes upon the Grail Castle.

Prior to this sudden memory, Perceval's actions mirrored those of contemporary men and women who have been taken up with efforts to become who they aspire to be in the world, or to achieve what it is they want for themselves. In focusing on their own goals, they may act as callously as Perceval toward people who loved, nurtured, or helped them on the way up, leaving them behind without so much as a backward glance. The ability to do so is part of the psychology of the hero, which emphasizes separation from the mother and the motherworld, denial of dependency, and corresponding intolerance for vulnerability, equated with weakness. Devaluation of feminine affiliative values and women readily follows.

Goal-focused women often do the same, especially if in their psychological typology they have the qualities of the mythical Athena. As you'll recall, Athena was born out of her father Zeus's head, with no memory of her mother Metis, the pre-Olympian goddess of wisdom. Metis had been swallowed by Zeus after being tricked into becoming small. Athena is often portrayed as a grown woman in armor, as a female knight. She is the patron deity of heroes.

Contemporary Athenas are women who do well in a man's world, where their intelligence, their ability to strategize and find mentors, and their ease at working with or competing with ambitious, bright men put them on a success track in the academic, corporate, or professional world. They wear intellectual armor and can focus on being productive and be unaware of their feelings, vulnerabilities, physical yearnings, or emotional needs. An Athena is a "father's daughter" who seeks to please "father"—her own father, or father figures—or gain patriarchal recognition for her achievements, until she "remembers mother." A dramatic pendulum swing may then take place when she realizes that the "mother" she forgot was her own instinctual feminine—has she lost the possibility of being Mother? With the intensity of a knight in search of the Grail, she may begin the quest to be a mother, which may take her into the emotional wilderness she walled herself off from and into the medical infertility maze, with its blind endings. The Grail she seeks is her own pregnant womb.

While the effort and anguish has to do with whether she is able to have a child, there is a destination that she is unconsciously seeking through the baby; it is the entry to the motherworld, Avalon. She seeks as much to be nurtured as to nurture. She wants to shed her intellectual armor and go home to find her lost feminine nature, which is much more than biological motherhood. She may find the Mother that nurtures her in Nature, in the company of women, in a trusting friendship; she may find the Mother in herself, or in a soul-nourishing activity.

Looked at metaphorically, remembering mother and returning to the forest to find her has many levels of meaning. Psychologically, it might happen when a grown son or daughter suddenly develops a loving insight and appreciation for his or her mother; he or she might, for instance, literally return home to let her know and in doing so initiate a deeper level of relationship with her. It might mean becoming aware of the mother archetype within, which is what is happening when a professional woman finds herself yearning to have a child and is suddenly able to turn away from the career track.

The mother archetype is also usually present when we fall in love with someone who is also in love with us and in the initial glow feel unconditionally loved, basking like a cherished child in the love of a mother. The endearments that lovers say to each other in "baby talk" are expressions of this unconscious connection. This is the maternal Eros of Aphrodite, whose symbolic red rose is the flower of lovers.

To remember mother and seek to find her again refers also to that sudden recollection of a world and an identity we left behind in childhood. For we each have a personal "prehistoric time," before we could write or tell time, before we knew about the calendar. If we experienced the mother archetype—in the form of our own mother or mother figure—as a positive force, we were in the mother realm of imagination, unconditional love, timelessness, and closeness to benevolent nature and instinct. (If our experience of mother was negative, or if we were unmothered, it could have instead been a time filled with fear and helplessness.) This is the world that the hero (as the ego in us all) has to leave behind when we go to school and then to work in a patriarchal culture that requires and rewards us for objectivity and rational thinking, goal focus and productivity.

Perceval worked at becoming a famous knight by winning conflicts or competitions with other men in armor. He either killed his opponents or, more usually, sent them back to Camelot as evidence of his success. In whatever field a person sets out to gain proficiency and recognition, there are analogous experiences, victories, or badges to win that are signs of success. After a while the challenge and satisfaction of doing the same thing over and over—be it making a sale or getting a promotion or winning a court case, all of which are contemporary versions of the competition between knights—loses its appeal. When it does, our energy for the task fizzles. This is the point where men and achieving women wonder, "Is this all there is?" It is at this point that we may experience a new openness to the inner world of feelings, thoughts, yearnings, memories. So it was for Perceval, who now remembered his mother and set out to find her again.

The Grail Castle

In the legend as first told by Chrétien de Troyes, Perceval then rides along until he comes to a deep river and supposes his mother's house must be somewhere on the far bank, but there is no crossing and the road he is on leads no farther. Then, as if in answer to a prayer, he catches sight of a boat with two men in it floating downstream. They drop anchor in the middle of the river, and one of them begins to fish. Perceval calls to them, asking if they know where he can cross or find shelter. In the story, as in life, the very act of seeking sets something in motion to meet us; something in the universe or in the unconscious responds as if to an invitation.

The fisherman first tells him that there is no ferry, bridge, or ford, no way to cross on horseback, and no boat large enough to carry a horse and rider, for twenty leagues up or down the river. However, the fisherman promises Perceval that if he rides up by a cleft in a rock to the top of the hill, he will see a house where he can find lodging that night.

At the top of the hill, Perceval gazes for a long time and sees nothing except sky and earth. He feels tricked and stupid. The next instant, he spies the tower of a huge castle. Descending into the valley, he approaches the castle and crosses the drawbridge. Suddenly he sees something he could not see before, and he finds an entrance to what turns out to be the Grail Castle. He comes "to that other world which corresponds to the mother . . . the realm of dreams and visions . . . an other worldly domain indicated by a change in atmosphere, which in contrast to previous events, now becomes magical" (the psychological interpretation of the Grail Castle in *The Grail Legend* by Emma Jung and Marie-Louise von Franz).

Once inside, Perceval is welcomed by the wounded lord of the castle, who is the same man who was fishing, though he now appears as a king. He is reclining and apologizes for not being able to rise to greet him because of the wound. He invites Perceval to sit at his side. Perceval is royally received, waited upon, and honored, and partakes of a magnificent banquet, during which marvels pass before him. Not just once, but with every course, he watches the Grail procession go by.

Grail Experiences

First a page enters carrying a white lance. From the tip of the lance, a drop of blood runs down the shaft to his hand. Two more pages follow, each carrying a golden candelabra lit with many candles. Between them walks the Grail-bearer, a beautiful maiden, splendidly garbed, holding the Grail between her two hands. As she enters the hall with the Grail, the light from it is so brilliant that the candles lose their brightness. A second woman carrying a silver platter follows. The lance that bleeds is usually part of Grail processions; it is supposedly the weapon used by the Roman soldier to wound Jesus in his side when he hung on the cross. The second woman who carries the platter in the procession is associated with the Goddess and her cauldron of plenty, while the Grail is both the cup of the Last Supper and a goddess symbol. Christian and goddess symbols overlap in the Grail legends, which may be why the Church never recognized them.

Though Perceval is in the midst of a wondrous, numinous experience, he makes no mention of it and asks no questions about what he is witnessing. Nor does he ask his host anything about his infirmity. Instead, he puts his mind on eating and drinking, even as the procession goes by time and again. After the meal, he passes the evening in inconsequential talk with the lord of the castle and then goes to bed. Perceval does not ask any questions or comment upon the extraordinary events because he is following the advice of his mentor, a nobleman who taught him the rudiments of being a knight and cautioned him not to reveal his ignorance by asking questions.

There are moments of great mystery that seem to pass by like the Grail procession in the lives of many people.

Liminal experiences at the threshold between worlds are not that uncommon; they are archetypal, mystical moments when we see through or beyond ordinary reality. People hear celestial music, see or feel what they call angelic presences, may have comforting or awesome visions, have an insight or intuition of unusual intensity, feel held by the Goddess, or sense the Goddess or God in themselves. They may be forever changed as a result of the experience, or the wonder and meaning of it may not touch them at all. And like Perceval, they may not even mention it.

I am convinced that most people have had "Grail experiences" sometime in their lives; they have had epiphanies, sacred moments, numinous or revelatory experiences, and have felt momentarily whole and healed, loved, touched by, or part of divinity or of the universe. The moment passes; as a result, either the course of that person's life changes or the moment has about as much impact as an exceptional meal.

The Grail experience itself is not enough. The question "Whom does the Grail serve?" needs to be answered. An experience of the Grail, like a vision imbued with meaning, can serve to deepen the soul, or not. In the presence of the Grail, Perceval makes small talk because he is afraid to look ignorant; his experience is shallow and he misses the meaning.

The next morning, Perceval awakens, walks past closed doors that won't open when he knocks, shouts to get attention, and gets no response. Then he leaves the castle and finds his horse saddled, his lance and shield leaning against the wall. He mounts and searches about the courtyard and again sees no one. Finally, he rides to the gate and finds the drawbridge lowered; as he begins to cross, the drawbridge rises. His horse makes a great leap and barely manages to clear the moat. He calls out, this time to whomever raised the drawbridge, but no one answers.

Once Perceval is out of the Grail Castle, the castle itself disappears. Perceval finds himself lost and nearly frozen in a forest, where he wanders for years seeking to find the Grail Castle again.

Perceval had become a successful knight, which took innate ability, effort, courage, ambition, and skill. After a time, the work that had been inspired and challenging became routine and was no longer a source of meaning. In this common midlife situation, he remembered his mother and set out to find her. In this, he heeded an inner feeling that called him to seek what he had left behind. This was an allegorical task; he did not know the way and there were no roads for him to follow. In this time of search, he unintentionally and unknowingly entered the otherworld, saw the Grail, and failed to acknowledge even seeing it, much less find out what it meant.

Contemporary Percevals, women as well as men, may also unintentionally encounter the otherworld during unsettled times of transition; we then may come in contact with the unconscious through dreams, synchronistic events, and projections onto others. If we have a Grail experience and then lose it because we failed to understand the importance to us of having this dimension in our lives, we often cannot go back to and be satisfied with the life we had before. Unsettled within ourselves, we find that we now are lost and wandering, like Perceval, "in the forest."

NINE

In the Forest: Midlife Landscape

*In the mid-path of my life, I woke to find myself
in a dark wood.*

DANTE, the beginning of *The Divine Comedy*

Ln dreams and literature,
events often occur in landscapes that serve as metaphors
for the emotional and spiritual terrain. Once out of the

Grail Castle, Perceval was lost in the forest, as are many of us at midlife. We find ourselves "in the forest" when we have lost our usual bearings: when we find ourselves questioning the meaning of what we are doing or who we are with, or have serious doubts about the path we have followed or the turn we took at the last crossroad.

We may lose what we once assumed was a permanent occupation or relationship, and with this also the familiar shelter of our usual place in the world, and find ourselves "in the forest." The forest, the labyrinth, the otherworld, the underworld, the sea, and the depths of the sea are all poetic and symbolic descriptions of how we perceive the unconscious as a realm. It is where we are when we are lost, and it is where we need to go in order to find ourselves. Individuation, the need to live from our own depths in an authentic and growing way, is a journey that takes the ego into the forest.

Being in the midst of the forest is a commentary upon a period of our lives. Down-home expressions refer to it as "being in the soup" or "not yet out of the woods." It is a time and metaphoric place of danger and transformation. There are no clearly marked signs or roads. If we are afraid, the shadows can seem ominous; if we are foolhardy, the forest can be a dangerous place.

Sometimes we unintentionally walk into the forest ourselves. Attracted by someone or something, we leave our familiar ground by changing or leaving relationships, work, family, community, or belief system. Sometimes we find ourselves in the forest because someone leaves us, or we lose a job, or because a medical diagnosis or accident changes everything.

There are also times when we find ourselves in the forest after intentionally ending some phase of our life; we walk through a door and shut it behind us, which takes us here. It is not enough to know that we must leave—a destructive relationship, job, environment; we must be able to act upon that knowledge. As in the Psyche myth, one must have both a lamp (a symbol of illumination or consciousness that allows us to see the situation clearly) and a knife (the power to act decisively, to be able to sever bonds).

The inability for life to go on as usual comes about for any number of reasons. It is not the event itself that does it but the depths into which our souls go as a result.

When we enter a forest phase in our lives, we enter a period of wandering and a time of potential soul growth. In the forest it is possible to reconnect with our own innate nature, to meet what we have kept in the shadows and what we have been kept from knowing or acknowledging about ourselves, or the personal and patriarchal world we inhabit. Here it is possible to find what we have been cut off from, to "re-member" a once vital aspect of ourselves. We may uncover a wellspring of creativity that has been hidden for decades. Here we may also be attacked by criticism or abandoned to our worst fears. Most of all, once in the forest, we must find within ourselves whatever we need to survive.

The Handless Maiden in the Forest:
Becoming Competent on One's Own

Like the handless maiden in the fairy tale of the same name, whose hands grew back while she was in the forest, many women find that it is only when they are on their own, unsupported and lost in unfamiliar territory, that analogous psychological growth occurs. Young women metaphorically let their hands be cut off to comply with what it means to be "appropriately feminine." Whereas preadolescent girls speak their minds easily and can be exuberant, assertive, and able to compete with boys, adolescent girls typically lose their self-esteem and refrain from self-expression.

Hands represent competency, the capacity to reach for and hold on to what is personally of value; hands are the means through which we can express feelings of intimacy and sensuality; hands are used to create, to comfort others and heal; hands get dirty when we muck around in soil or machinery, or enter shadowy transactions; hands hold musical instruments, paintbrushes, cooking implements, tools, and weapons; hands protect us, fulfill curiosity, and are in their many ways extensions of our psyches into the world. Hands have to do with self-esteem and self-expression both actually and metaphorically.

To understand how "The Handless Maiden" might be a story with personal meaning, muse upon your own inhibitions or limitations. Might a particular set of "hands" have been cut off?

Growing hands that never developed or were cut off is especially necessary for a woman who goes from her father's house to her husband's, and then, following his death or incapacitation or, most commonly, a divorce, must go out into the world and support herself, or herself and others. She is like the handless maiden, unskilled and on her own.

If she has been raised to be a lady, there are always parts of her personality that are stunted or cut off: she has learned not to express anger, strong opinions, or say what is on her mind. Abilities and personality traits that were not welcomed were not developed. She was made to feel ashamed of any parts of herself that were unbecoming, and, consequently, these aspects were repressed—or cut off.

In the fairy tale, a miller makes a deal with the devil to give him whatever is behind the millhouse in exchange for riches and status. When he comes home, he finds that his daughter had been sweeping behind the millhouse, and that it is she whom he has promised to the devil. The first time the devil comes to collect, the daughter's innocence and purity prevents him from taking possession of her. He tells the miller and his wife that they must keep the daughter from caring for herself so that when he next comes to claim her, she will be disheveled and dirty. However, her copious tears cleanse her hands, which prevents him from taking her. Angry and determined not to relinquish his claim, which he must do if he fails the third time, the devil tells the miller to cut off his daughter's hands, which the father does. When the devil returns to claim the handless maiden, her tears fall upon the stumps, and their purity repels the devil. The maiden then refuses to be dependent upon the material security that her parents offer, and she chooses instead to go out into the world handless and alone. She would rather trust the generosity of strangers than remain where she is.

In myth, legend, and fairy tales, father figures agree to trade beautiful, young, innocent maidens for power and success. In patriarchal cultures, daughters are often expendable, violated, their development thwarted, their wishes and needs ignored. It is no wonder the theme recurs in stories. In the psyches of men (and increasingly in women as well), feminine values and expression of feelings are often repressed because they are incompatible with the acquisition of power. Thus the theme of sacrificing the maiden as a metaphor for feminine values and innocence rings psychologically true. In families that expect girl children to go from being obedient daughters to obedient wives, talents and traits that do not fit these expectations are metaphorically cut off.

The part of the story of the handless maiden that takes place in a forest corresponds to the psychological terrain that women are in when we are on our own and in a time of major transition in our lives. It is a time when we can discover what matters to us and what gives our lives meaning, and a time in which necessity is a stimulus to growth, as we cope with new responsibilities and challenges. The forest segment of the fairy tale takes place after the handless maiden has married, given birth to her baby, and must flee. With her newborn daughter strapped across her breasts, she enters the forest. She spends seven years in the forest, and in Clarissa Pinkola Estés's version in *Women Who Run with the Wolves,* her hands grow back in stages. First they are baby hands, then the hands of a girl, and finally she has the hands of the whole woman she has become.

The handless maiden with her newborn strapped across her breasts is a symbolic figure similar to the pregnant Psyche in the Greek myth of Eros and Psyche. New life is represented by the new child. In this story Psyche is a beautiful woman who has been abandoned by Eros, the god of love (the Greek word *psyche* means "soul"; it is also the name for butterfly, which in metamorphosing from caterpillar through chrysalis to butterfly is a symbol of transformation). In order to grow, Psyche must complete four tasks; each one seems impossible until helpers come to her aid—ants, a reed, an eagle, and a talking tower (all symbols for qualities within her).

The tasks represent what the feminine psyche must learn in order to grow. On completion of each of the four tasks, the woman who identifies with Psyche or the handless maiden has become competent psychologically in ways she was not before. When she accomplishes the first task of sorting a vast number of different seeds into separate mounds, a woman acquires the ability to sort out possibilities, to make order out of confusion, to learn that she has the psychological, intellectual, or intuitive means to sort out and make sense of what she faces when she is on her own.

Psyche's second task is to acquire some fleece from the golden rams of the sun, which are huge, aggressive rams that butt heads as they competitively fight for dominance. She has to find a way of getting a symbol of power for herself without being trampled or destroyed in the effort. This is the same task a woman must do when she goes out into the competitive world and must fend for herself. She has to learn to acquire the power she needs without losing her soul and becoming tough, unrelated to others, and out of touch with her feelings and values.

Psyche's third task requires her to gain the overview perspective of an eagle as well as the eagle's ability to discriminate and grasp what it wants. When a woman has learned this, she has gained the ability to see patterns and act decisively on her own behalf.

The fourth and last task requires Psyche to enter the underworld and return with a box filled with precious ointment. She can accomplish this only because she is able to say no to those who want her to help them. She gains the ability to do what every woman must learn to do. When we rescue people or do for them, and the cost of doing so traps us in fulfilling their needs and not our own, our growth becomes stunted, and we are cut off from the possibility of becoming whole ourselves. We become like handless maidens who agree to have parts of ourselves cut off, when we are in codependent relationships and denial. Only when we are able to say no can our yes be true and unequivocal.

Perceval in the Forest: A Place Where the Soul Can Grow

Perceval spent more than five years wandering in the forest, as did other knights in quest of the Grail. The knight who becomes lost and cold in the forest has tasks that are far different from the handless maiden's. Like men and women who get caught up in appearances and worldly success and then in midlife find themselves in the forest, the knight must realize what he has failed to do or did not value sufficiently and lost. Perceval saw the wound that would not heal and ignored what he saw, which was a failure of compassion. He saw the Grail procession and remained unaffected, staying in his persona. The forest is a place of soul growth for people who are Percevals, a time to learn about suffering and compassion, humility and humiliation, feminine wisdom and the mysterious Grail.

In the forest, Perceval encountered many people and puzzling situations. He met a weeping maiden crying over a warrior whose head had been cut off, an ill-treated maiden on a wretched nag, a loathsome damsel hideous to behold, a hermit in a chapel, a black knight lying in a tomb, a dead knight lying on an altar, a mysterious woman wearing a red robe strewn with stars, a child in a tree of lights. He encountered animals, among which were a dangerous white stag, a black-and-white horse, a pure white horse, and a white dog on a gold leash. He was challenged to a chess game, decided to hunt the stag, released a knight in a tomb. As in dreams, some figures were helpful, others were hostile or neutral toward him, and all of the characters and situations could be interpreted symbolically.

People in the midst of a forest period can discover that what they encounter are projections or synchronistic meetings; what we may find lovely or loathsome in others are likely qualities or attitudes that exist in us. Likewise we may be that loathsome damsel, headless knight, or weeping maiden to someone else—or even to ourselves.

Artemis in the Forest: Getting in Touch with the Wilderness

The forest was a realm of the Greek goddess Artemis (or Diana), who was the Goddess of the Hunt and the Moon. Artemis is an archetype present in women who are spiritually nurtured by Mother Nature and instinctually attuned to their own wilderness nature. As a virgin goddess archetype, Artemis is a "one-unto-herself," independent spirit. Many of us are archetypally Artemis before the double impact of puberty and patriarchy makes us "handless maidens." She's also an embodied archetype; she is in the little girl who climbs trees and can be resurrected by a woman who once again becomes physically active in the outdoors.

We are uncomfortable with, or reject or are ashamed of, any part of us that is not welcomed in our world and are likely to cut ourselves off from whatever it is about us that others do not like, think inappropriate, or are uncomfortable with, if we can. These are the parts of us that we didn't develop or we suppressed, forgot, and lost touch with that may be sources of vitality and meaning. Any archetype that we have cut ourselves off from is alive in the forest of our unconscious. As the only goddess who came to the aid of her mother as well as looking out for the young of all living things, Artemis as an archetype represents the part of a woman who has a genuine and deep connection with the earth and who may act from her love and her outrage to protect forests, animals, women and children, the planet, and vulnerable parts of herself.

Robert Bly in *Iron John* encourages men to reclaim the archetype of the wild man, and Clarissa Pinkola Estés writes about reconnecting with a corresponding wild woman archetype; they are instinctual parts of ourselves that we need in order to be fully alive. During midlife, the desire to be real to ourselves, which comes from our soul, contributes to the crises we unconsciously create when we do not consciously acknowledge that we do not feel vital and authentic. There is an internal impetus to become a whole person and when we spend time in the metaphorical forest *and* the actual forest or natural world, we are exposed to the possibility of retrieval and growth of our instinctual nature, our spiritual connection with Nature, and our sense of oneness with the universe.

The Forest as a Labyrinth Experience

In the midpath of my life, I left my marriage and entered a
period of being in a dark wood. It took me a while to understand that in this forest I couldn't climb a tree, get an
overview, or see where I was headed and go there. I couldn't
influence the warmth or coldness of the emotional weather,
or change the circumstances and people I encountered in
the forest. I learned to accept whatever happened, however
unexpected or disappointing, and would say to myself,
"Whatever is, is." I gradually accepted that I really was
alone here. I learned about living in the immediate present.

Life in the midst of the forest existed side by side with
the tasks of ordinary life: I was the mother of two adolescent children who lived with me half of the time and were
having their own difficulties. I was a psychiatrist with
many commitments. There were all the usual details of
life, from school conferences to shopping to paying taxes.
In addition, because I had done the leaving, separation en-
tailed moving and reorganizing a great deal of my life,
from taking charge of my finances to filling a bare cup-
board beginning with staples and spices.

While I knew I was in pain about what was happening, I could put it aside to take care of all there was to
cope with. Like many therapists, I focused on the other
people in my life, on how they were reacting and why. Intellectual understanding was my armor; I went into my
head and was out of touch with the tension, fear, and
confusion that my body carried for me. In this forest pe-

riod of my life, I was gradually learning to attend to the perceptions and emotions held in my body. And there were the added emotional encounters, which were hard and also, on balance, very deepening and real. A separation is very hard on those who have no say in its happening and yet are greatly affected. Our marriage had looked like a stable rock, and now it was as if that rock had been thrown into a pool, creating concentric rings of emotional reactivity in others.

At times, it was a struggle to stay aware and responsible in the ordinary world, with the forest exerting an emotional pull inward, for however painful it is, there is vitality in the midst of living in the archetypal world, or even in being cast in one's own version of a soap opera.

Until I entered the "in the forest" phase of my life, I had been on a well-established and well-traveled road with objective signposts and obvious destinations. There was a sequence and a time frame to education and professional accomplishments. So many years and requirements passed to get the B.A., then the M.D., licensure, boards in psychiatry and neurology; certification as a Jungian analyst upon completion of a lengthy training program; up the academic ladder, step by step, until I reached the top as clinical professor. Each step was marked by ceremonies or public recognition of some kind. Personal decisive events were occasions for wedding and birth announcements, as they, too, were established institutions.

Once off the well-paved and maintained road, I had indeed awakened to find myself in a dark wood. Now I found the markers were almost entirely subjective and symbolic; my interpretations of dreams and events served as compasses or signs about the meaning of where I was. Synchronistic events became more symbolically significant than my dreams; my dreams seemed to become less important in this unfamiliar psychological terrain through which I had to find my own way. Major synchronicities (Mrs. Detiger's gift of this pilgrimage was one) now took the place of "big" dreams.

Some of the most significant of these symbolically coincidental events occurred on my birthday, which made them synchronicities: a birthday marks the beginning of a brand new year for the birthday person, not for everybody. Each birthday brings with it the potentiality of a new beginning, new or renewed life, a symbolic new birth or rebirth, as well as marking the passage, the end, or the symbolic death of the previous year. When I left my husband, I also left our home and found temporary shelters, places to stay that provided a roof over my head for the next several months. I decided that I would look for a condominium, which would be a temporary and practical solution. When I found the right place the first day I looked, the decision felt as if it had been supported by circumstance. I could not move in, however, until the sellers found another place, which happened about three months later. The day the condominium became mine and I would move in turned out to fall on my birthday, which felt like a synchronicity; the move marked a new beginning, and a second event on this same day made clear that it also marked a sad end. On the morning of my birthday, Rainbow, our family dog, died. That afternoon, my husband, our children, and I buried her in the yard. That night, my children and I would spend the first night in sleeping bags in the living room of my new house. I think that animals are deeply connected to the instinctual, emotional lives of their people and that in some way, she sacrificed herself for us and was thus the scapegoat or sacrificial animal that carried or expressed the pain of our disintegrating family; maybe she developed a malignancy in place of one of us.

Divorce is another major marker, the only one during an "in the forest" phase that is a public statement as well as a significant internal event. I do not think that it is ever just a legal formality; something also shifts in the inner world and the morphic field. A connection is severed (or helped to be severed) that otherwise holds a person back like an invisible cord binding her or him to the past and to an old identity, preventing the person from moving into the next phase of life, which may not even have to do with ever being in another relationship. Going through a divorce brings people into dark places in the forest; we go into dark and shadowy psychological places in ourselves and are exposed to dark and shadowy parts of the spouse we are divorcing. Decisions have to be made; how will we respond? We encounter economic, social, and psychological fears that sometimes are at survival level, and must acknowledge the death of the dream that we once shared and the disintegration of an image we had of ourselves and of the person we married. On a psychological level, a divorce is the equivalent of entering surgery for a potentially life-threatening condition; it takes us into the underworld, where we must face fears for our survival, a procedure that has risks in itself and one we must recuperate from afterward.

We did not enter divorce proceedings immediately and I was not divorced until exactly three years after the birthday that was marked by the death of our family dog and my new residence; the date that was stamped on the papers that made the divorce official was my birthday. The timing struck me in several ways; it felt uncanny and synchronistic, meaningful and affirming of what it was I was doing. I believe that I was the first person in a multigenerational extended large family on both my mother's and my father's side to get a divorce, and it was not something I had anticipated as a possibility when I married. This shedding of the expectations of others and of myself was part of the forest experience.

I know that the very belief that I held that this journey had meaning, even when I could not see what it was, sustained me and shaped the nature of this passage. In the forest part of my life, I was in the process of becoming more authentic; I retreated from professional meetings and social occasions where I had to wear a persona or a social or professional face. I began recovering myself in the company of a few good friends and in being part of women's circles for the first time. I participated in individual psychotherapy, some couple work, and bodywork, and had the tools gained in the course of previous analysis and my own training. There were times when I used the *I Ching* or *The Book of Runes* to get a reading on where I was and what my attitude should be or what my lessons were; they provide a wisdom perspective and are oracular means to reflect upon our circumstances. I increasingly prayed for guidance for myself and others and found that prayer became a regular spiritual practice.

While the "in the forest" time is a labyrinth experience, it is not clearly marked as in the labyrinth at Chartres. The pattern of entering, getting to the center, and coming out is, however, a map of the psychological process: shedding, finding, and integrating. Going into the forest requires us to let go of our old ways and identities; we shed defenses, ingrained habits, and attitudes, which opens us up to new possibilities and depth. We find what really matters to us and can reach the core or center of meaning in ourselves, which is the center of the labyrinth, and then we have the task of integrating this into what we do with our lives when we emerge.

Seven years after entering the forest phase of my life, I had a deep urge to move. I heeded my internal timing and found the perfect house for me and settled in. My intuition was that I was moving into a more expansive period as well, and I looked forward to celebrating the birthday that followed this move as a new beginning, anticipating that it would mark a new phase of my life.

I was to meet three friends for a birthday dinner in the wine country north of San Francisco. I left my office early and headed up Highway 101 on a warm midafternoon and took the exit that leads to the Napa Valley. There is a portion of this road that is a long, level, multilaned straightaway, lined with telephone poles and with a wide ditch paralleling the highway and the railroad tracks beyond. It is an empty stretch of road, and the flow of traffic usually exceeds the speed limit. I was probably driving at least 60 MPH, when I fell asleep at the wheel. I woke up with my car moving through tall weeds that were hitting my windshield; it felt like I was in a dream. I was disoriented about whether I was dreaming and where I was, and it took me a moment to know that I was awake and in my car and that I had better put my foot on the brake. Within minutes after the car stopped, two very concerned men ran down the embankment to see if I was all right. They were Good Samaritans who had come to help, and witnesses to what had happened. When I fell asleep at the wheel, I was in the outside lane. The men said that they were right behind me and saw my car headed straight for a telephone pole, and that I had missed it by only three or four feet. Once my car got onto the sloping shoulder of the highway, that slight inclination must have altered the course I had been on. I barely missed the pole and went off the road, down the embankment, and into the ditch between the highway and the raised railroad track. My car traveled then for more than a hundred yards before it stopped.

When I realized how close a call it had been, it felt as if I had had guardian angels looking after me, and as if these men who on a long empty stretch of highway had immediately stopped to help were human guardian angels as well. They were part of my birthday present; I had been given my life, as I had the day I was born. It was another birthday synchronicity. It dramatically marked the end of the period of being in the forest and clearly heralded a new beginning.

Out of the Woods

Perceval spent over five years in the forest, the handless maiden seven, which is often how long it takes for people on an individuation journey to "get out of the woods" and fully into the next phase of their lives. Like every other labyrinthine process, it takes as long as it takes. Only after we make it out, do we know how it has changed us, what we shed and left behind, and what we gave birth to, found, or recovered there.

This "in the soup" time can then indeed be appreciated as a cauldron of rebirth and regeneration, the Celtic cauldron that was a precursor to the Christian Grail, that contained pain and darkness as well as beauty and mystery, from which it is possible to emerge in some significant way transformed.

As scary as it can be in the midst of the forest, as long and as alone as we may be there, it is a psychological landscape that is alive and full of potential. It is a far better place for the soul to be than in the wasteland.

THE JOURNEY

One day you finally knew
what you had to do, and began,
though the voices around you
kept shouting
their bad advice—
though the whole house
began to tremble
and you felt the old tug
at your ankles.
"Mend my life!"
each voice cried.
But you didn't stop.
You knew what you had to do,
though the wind pried
with its stiff fingers
at the very foundations—
though their melancholy
was terrible.
It was already late
enough, and a wild night,
and the road full of fallen
branches and stones.

In the Forest: Midlife Landscape

But little by little,
as you left their voices behind,
the stars began to burn
through the sheets of clouds,
and there was a new voice,
which you slowly
recognized as your own,
that kept you company
as you strode deeper and deeper
into the world,
determined to do
the only thing you could do—
determined to save
the only life you could save.

MARY OLIVER, *Dream Work*

The Wasteland:
Depression and Despair

I n the Grail legend, the Fisher King has a wound that will not heal, and his kingdom is a wasteland. Only if the Grail heals him will the kingdom be restored and come to life again. The wasteland is a metaphor for a barren psychological landscape where creativity and generativity are absent, where nothing grows and life is meaningless and emotionally flat. As metaphor, the wasteland is also a real-life human experience that can be vividly, terrifyingly real. This was the situation for two men who consulted me and whose stories I tell because there are echoes of their stories in the lives of many midlife men and women.

Feeling Unreal: Depersonalization as an Emotional Wasteland

One man told me of his repetitive nightmares. In these dreams, his surroundings were ordinary enough; nothing in them was threatening or explicitly dangerous. What made them nightmares didn't have to do with events, but with the absence of familiarity, with not being himself. It was not that he had amnesia—in the dreams, he had no problem knowing who or where he was. The anguish had to do with not *feeling* who he was.

As I listened, I intuitively felt myself in his place, which is how I often work with dreams, and I was reminded of patients who experience depersonalization in waking life. People with this symptom feel alarmingly unreal, sometimes so much so that they cut themselves to be reassured that they bleed and therefore must be alive. When I equated this with his dream, he was relieved to have a concept, to have words for his condition, and to be understood.

The nightmares temporarily stopped, coinciding with the visit of his sister, with whom he could talk about what really mattered to him. She loved him and "bore witness" to his life. With her, he was able to talk about himself and feel understood as he struggled to find a way "to be real" and yet to fulfill what his family and position in life required of him. Without her he was isolated. No one else considered his difficulties a legitimate source of anguish.

He was a man with the soul of a poet who went into business, as was expected of him. At midlife, his fortunes had taken a turn for the worse. The business that he had never had his heart in anyway was failing, and as he put more effort into it, he felt increasingly unreal.

Depersonalization is a symptom of some severity that is related to feeling inauthentic, to identifying with the persona or mask one wears, or the role one plays, or the effort to conform to what others expect, while burying what one really feels or knows to be true, or denying what is really personally important.

I could understand personally how one comes to feel inauthentic and unreal. I have thought of this as an occupational hazard of being a psychiatrist and an emotional hazard of being a supportive wife, as well. In both roles I focused on how someone else was feeling and I stifled my own spontaneity, opinions, wishes, anger, and tears, which can contribute to feeling unreal.

Both men in general and professional women are expected to be objective rather than subjective. When we must hide our vulnerability and emotionality from others, we also distance ourselves from our own feelings and reactions. When we put a lid on our emotional expressiveness, we lose the ability to be spontaneous. Men have additional social pressures on them to conform to a cultural stereotype;

they are supposed to prefer competitive occupations where they can amass power or money, and they are expected to be successful at it. While some men are natural competitors who thrive in such situations, many men "fake it"; they work in occupations and professions that have very little intrinsic, personal meaning and, at the cost of becoming increasingly alienated from themselves, act as if they really care about what they are doing.

There is something liberating about hearing the truth that a dream is trying to get the dreamer to heed. It's more than just a feeling of being freer and lighter; often creative thinking is liberated and rapid connections are made. For example, when the man who had the depersonalization nightmares heard that it had to do with his being increasingly inauthentic and out of touch with what deeply mattered to him, something clicked for him. In his next breath, he asked me about the wounded king, the fool, and the Grail that he had read about in my book *The Tao of Psychology*. The poet in him made the connection; depersonalization had to do with suffering from the wound that would not heal and from being in the wasteland. His dream answered the question "What ails thee?" which he needed to know before any healing could take place. And because I was working on this very chapter when he unexpectedly asked about the Grail legend, it felt like a synchronistic event for me—an affirmation of what I was doing.

Synchronicities are soulful. It is the soul that knows something is meaningful, that is moved by poetry and music, that recognizes what it loves and that it is loved, that is nourished by what we do when what we do comes from our own depths. If virtually nothing that we do in daily life is soul satisfying, which is the situation out of which nightmares of depersonalization arise, we become increasingly unreal to ourselves.

Life Devoid of Life: The Wasteland of Meaninglessness

The second man's story was even more terrible. His "nightmare" was actually a waking experience that probably lasted only a matter of seconds. It had occurred four years earlier, at 2:00 P.M. on December 21. (Though he was unaware of it, December 21 is the winter solstice, the darkest time of the year; there could not have been a more symbolic date.) He was in a crosswalk near Union Square in San Francisco, in the midst of Christmas shoppers and holiday decorations, when suddenly he felt as if a motion picture had stopped and the scene had frozen. First motion and sound dropped away, and everyone and everything was suspended in a silent vacuum; then, as he watched in horror, all color drained out—it was like "watching the world suddenly bleed to death"—until everything was lifeless, immobile, and in shades of gray.

A moment later, everything was as it had been before. He hurried to catch up with his friend, who was walking in front of him, to say something about what he had just experienced. It was impossible to convey then what he had felt; for again, it was not what he had *seen* that was so awful, but what he had *felt*. Recollecting that moment, he said, "My experience was that the 'blood' was draining out of *everything;* no life was left at all, anywhere. That was the experience that haunted me for years: the conviction that there was no 'blood'—juice, meaning, life, joy—*anywhere.*"

He felt like he had gotten a glimpse of the ultimate reality, and it was empty, lifeless, meaningless. "This was what life really was like, what lay beyond the *maya,* or the illusion of life," he thought. In the years that followed, he might be with close friends having a good dinner, taking pleasure in their company, when the memory of that moment would come up and wash over the present and make it devoid of meaning. Or he might be driving down the California coast and in the midst of enjoying the beauty when the moment in the crosswalk would come back to him and take all joy away.

His life looked wonderful to others. He was one of several partners in a successful consulting firm, where mistrust and competitiveness among them had resulted in an atmosphere that was strained and at times even unpleasant. This, on top of the sense of existential meaninglessness that kept coming up when he remembered the moment in the crosswalk, was making life increasingly empty for him.

He had insomnia and the beginning of an ulcer. Once when he asked himself "What really is wrong?" the empty feeling of "Mommy's gone" came welling up from the time in his early childhood when his mother died.

Then a couple of months later, he had a heart attack at work. He didn't want to bother anybody, so he first told himself it was nothing, then that it was indigestion, or psychosomatic. But he could not ignore the pain in his heart. Hospitalization followed by heart surgery preceded his psychiatric consultation.

As I listened to his story, I was moved by the terrible sense of nothingness that he had felt in that moment and how his life had become increasingly without meaning ever since. He was a well-functioning, high-achieving person. Yet he was living with a profound sense of meaninglessness. He was in a Dark Night of the Soul.

Most depressions that take such a toll in spirit last for many, many months, while his was over in a matter of seconds, minutes at the most. I told him that it was the mystical opposite of illumination. It was an experience of "endarkenment" as profound in its capacity to affect him as an experience of enlightenment and subsequent recollection might be. That I could know how awful this was for him on a soul level proved to be a lifeline that reached to his soul. His particular spiritual path was taking him through the desert or wasteland; he was on the *via negativa*, the path where soul encounters negation and pain. Often when there are insights into the meaning of a situation, spontaneity comes into play and a twinkle in the eye signals a return to life. My patient could lament, "How come Shirley Maclaine gets to dance in the light?" paraphrasing the title of her then-current best-selling book about her *via positiva* spiritual path. His question was not irreverent; why some travel the *via positiva* while others must travel the *via negativa* is one of those unknowables.

"Mommy's Gone": Death Mother and Stone Mother

I thought of the upwelling of grief and pain that had accompanied the inner words "Mommy's gone" and how these words might be expressing what was now wrong with my patient's world. For a world without the divinity of Mother is a material world devoid of color and life, of matter devoid of meaning, a devitalized world, turned to stone.

His "Mommy's gone" feeling of anguish, coupled with the experience of lifelessness in that moment in the crosswalk, brought to mind the negative aspects of the Great Mother archetype. Two descriptions, one from the poet Robert Bly in *Sleepers Holding Hands,* the other from the author Lynn Andrews's description of "La Ultima Madre" in *Jaguar Woman,* aptly conveyed something to me that I could in turn pass on. I described the four faces of the Great Mother as I remembered them: the life-giving, Nurturing Mother and her opposite, the Death Mother; the Ecstatic or Dancing Mother and her opposite, the Stone Mother.

The wasteland world my client saw in the crosswalk was a world of the Stone Mother and the Death Mother.

I thought back to the time of my separation, when I could not handle the anger and accusations that my husband directed at me, or be in touch with the pain I was causing him, which his anger covered, or feel my own pain. I could neither retaliate in kind with anger, nor could I feel for him or myself. I was numbed, felt emotionally battered, and said it was akin to postconcussion syndrome. He said that I was stonewalling. In retrospect I was, at that moment, the Stone Mother and the Death Mother who no longer had feelings. My heart had turned to stone; it could not recognize him.

When the Nurturing and Dancing Mother leaves the world, an emotional wasteland results. In Greek mythology, Demeter, goddess of the Grain, the most giving and bountiful of the deities, who represented the Mother Goddess at a time when patriarchal religions were becoming predominant, became the Death Mother when she refused to let anything on earth grow and would have allowed humankind to die of famine. Her heart and compassion had turned to stone. She became the Stone Mother. The people of the earth could well have lamented, "Mother's gone!" as the inner child within my patient did.

I think of the newborns in the nursery who were fed and changed and kept warm and antiseptic but were not picked up to be hugged, touched, cooed at, or loved, and who died of what Dr. Bowlby, in his classic work, called "anaclitic depression." And of the unwanted and uncherished babies I had treated when I was an intern and medical student, who had been admitted to the pediatric wards of county hospitals with the diagnosis of "failure to thrive." These children often had depressed mothers—mothers in whom the archetypal Mother in her positive aspect was missing, women who were Stone Mothers and Death Mothers.

Child-rearing practices can simulate deprivation, though not to an extreme where failure to thrive physically results, but I do wonder how different we might be if maternal instinct alone determined how much physical contact mothers had with their babies. American infants were raised "by the book" for several decades by well-intentioned young mothers who read that babies were not to be picked up when they cried—lest they become spoiled; for similar character-building reasons, they were not to be fed when they were hungry either and instead had to adhere to four-hour intervals between bottles (unless the mother "weakened"). By following the expert advice of a male pediatrician, these mothers let their babies cry and denied their own instincts to the contrary, because they wanted to be good mothers. It left generations of infants who are now adults touch-deprived; Mother was not gone, but she was not responsive to them.

The babies in the nursery who died when no one lovingly touched them came into a world where Mother was gone, as did the older infants who failed to thrive. When elders become mentally confused and unable to take care of themselves, they become like lost children who need Mother. Touch is especially reassuring and affirming as it is with young children, and may even be life-sustaining when they are ill or feeble and depressed. It's as if a transfusion of energy is given when they are lovingly held at such times. Women caregivers who remember being mothers of young children feel the similarity in caring for the very young and very old; there is a similar depletion of energy and difficulty staying focused for them; a similar need for patience in helping an elder dress, bathe, or go over something repeatedly that he or she is trying to figure out that it takes to do this with a distractable child who has no sense of time.

The maternal matrix that women provide *is* life-sustaining, which is why widowers are known to be unusually susceptible to dying within a year of losing their wives. This also is an explanation for the devastating loss that many men feel when their wives leave them, and their often uncharacteristically irrational and even destructive behavior, which often has much more to do with the loss of this matrix ("Mother" has gone) than the loss of the particular woman herself. The power of the Goddess who manifests through women is an emotional matrix that invites unconscious merger or symbiosis and provides a sense of "coming home." If it is through women that many men receive some essential life-supporting ingredient for well-being, it makes sense that such men go to great lengths to control women, especially if they do not particularly like them and do not want to admit their dependency.

The Wounded Fisher King and the Wasteland

In the Grail legend, the wasteland can become green again if the ailing Fisher King's wound is healed by the Grail.

In the various Grail legends, the Fisher King's wound is in his thigh or genitals; hence wounded sexuality, creativity, and generativity are implied. In human life, we experience this wound when we're out of touch with what we're feeling, when we find ourselves lacking in spontaneity, when we're so concerned about productivity that we no longer value love, beauty, or play. These attitudes that put us out of touch are fostered by patriarchy with its emphasis on acquisition of power, leading to loss of soul and devaluation of the *anima* or the feminine in men.

Sexuality may then be expressed rotely or seen as a skill at which one becomes expert, or as an expression of power and domination. Creativity is inhibited by a critical, skeptical, denigrating, or perfectionistic judge, either as an inner figure or an outer one. Generativity is not fostered where exploitation or use of people as an expendable resource is the prevailing attitude. When the wounded and controlling king rules as an archetype over culture, family, or personality, eventually a wasteland results where nothing grows.

A king's mandate is to accumulate power and build secure defenses. These happen to be the ruling values in a patriarchal culture as well. Time and energy for personal feelings, play, sensuality, emotional bonding, the pleasures of discovery, enjoyment of the outdoors, expressiveness and individuality, friends of the heart, or the company of children are begrudged.

Being cut off from these sources of personal renewal eventually saps the ability to be creative, to enjoy sexuality and sensuality, to be playful or loving. "When is there time?" is the lament, especially in the career-track years. Only if our heart is in the work and we are either doing work we love or are with people we love will creativity and play be a part of our work life. And when most of the hours of the day are spent away from our families or personal intimates, deprivation may make what should be a source of emotional nourishment feel like one more demand.

The wounded Fisher King sitting in the midst of the wasteland is a metaphor for midlife depression for men and women who become caught up in acquiring position and power. In the rigorously scheduled, productive patriarchal world measured by Father Time, we suffer the lack of the kind of nourishing activities in which we lose track of time—when we can play or just enjoy being instead of doing. A flat, dry depression results; there are no tears or grief; existence is joyless.

Since wounds to the thigh or leg prevent a man from standing, they can be symbolically interpreted as meaning that a person is not grounded. To be "ungrounded" is to be unrealistically out of touch with material reality (*material* is derived from *mater/mother*) or not related to the instinctual world or the embodied world or the natural world or the soulful world. It commonly means that someone is living in his or her head rather than in his or her body.

In one version of the Grail legend, the king had been so badly wounded in battle that he couldn't ride or walk, so that fishing was his only pastime, and hence his name, the Fisher King. Another version of the legend speaks of the king as an old and ailing man who has outlived his time and is awaiting the coming of an heir before he can die. In all versions of the legend, there is an ailing king and a wasteland that can be restored only when the king is healed by the Grail.

The Grail Maiden and the Goddess

The Grail that Perceval seeks, the Grail that can heal the king, the Grail that disappeared from the world is in the possession of the Grail Maiden, who carries it in the Grail procession. If an innocent knight sees it and asks what ails the king or inquires whom the Grail serves, then, according to legend, the king will be healed by the Grail and the wasteland will be restored.

There is a mythological parallel between the wasteland of the Grail legend and the devastated earth that would no longer bring forth new life until an angry and grieving Demeter got her daughter Persephone back from the underworld. Persephone and the Grail Maiden are similar symbols: spring, the return of greenness to the earth, will come through them. Their disappearance is a cause of aridity and a lack of life; their reappearance reanimates a dead land.

Persephone, in her myth as the abducted goddess, was called the Kore or the Maiden. She, like the Grail Maiden, was nameless. I think this fits who they really were: the Maiden aspect of the once-revered Great Goddess, who was trinitarian as Maiden, Mother, Crone, whose worship was suppressed by followers of patriarchal gods, Judeo-Christian and Muslim.

Persephone was abducted by Hades, king of the underworld. The Grail Maiden might be considered similarly captive in the Grail Castle. Both disappeared from the world. Though Persephone was captive in the underworld, over which Hades ruled, he could not make her love him. The Grail King is in a similar position. Though he is lord of the castle, the Grail that would heal him, which the Grail Maiden carries, is beyond his power to demand.

Both the Fisher King and Hades rule kingdoms that have no life. Their kingdoms are a wasteland and a dead land. Only if Persephone returns to her grieving mother, Demeter, will the Earth be fruitful once more. Only if a knight enters the Grail Castle and says what needs to be said will the Grail heal the king and restore the wasteland. Only if these conditions are met will Mother Nature, Demeter, the Goddess reanimate the barren kingdom. Only then will the Mother Goddess return and function once more. The Maiden carries the Grail, which is the healing, nurturing vessel, and a symbolic representation of the Goddess. The Kore has to be reunited with the Mother, who can function once more as provider of greenness to the earth, of agriculture, and giver of the Mystery religion whose initiates "no longer feared death."

The Goddess of the Druidic British Isles and the Goddess of Old Europe are one and the same. When we humans—

with the exception of some indigenous peoples, such as Native Americans—stopped honoring her, we also lost our connection to the earth as sacred, ceased to be attuned to the seasons and to all life, ceased to have an embodied spirituality. With the domination of Sky Father gods, dominion over the Earth and all life (including women) was considered a divine right of men, who were supposedly created in the image of God. However, in the symbolic language of myth, knowledge of the suppressed Goddess was kept alive, just as dreams "remember" in symbolic language what the ego suppresses.

Meaninglessness and depression often follow this disconnection from the Grail or the Goddess. For this wasteland to be restored, the individual must reestablish a vital connection with Mother Nature or the Mother Goddess or mother archetype in her positive aspect. That vital connection is symbolized by Persephone the Kore or by the Grail Maiden. For women, the Maiden is the sacred daughter of the Great Mother, through whom women have an inner sense that divinity and femininity are linked. For men, the Maiden is another name for the anima or soul image, Jung's label for the feminine in men.

Midlife Depressions

Midlife depressions are manifestations of the wounded Fisher King and the Stone Mother. The king is ailing and passively waits in the Grail Castle, his kingdom a wasteland. Demeter, in her anger and depression, sits in her temple like a stone, unmoved by suffering, famine, and pleas to return life to the earth.

Unless their souls are nourished by other parts of their lives, men and women who work at jobs they do not like just for the paycheck often find themselves suffering from midlife Fisher King depressions.

Men and women who devote their lives to their work simply or primarily to gain recognition or money or power, to please others, or to live up to their own or family expectations also find themselves in midlife Fisher King depressions, especially if they do not rise as high as they anticipated and aren't well rewarded for the work done. Under the depression, they are angry and resentful. When people devote the better part of their lives to unrewarding work, depression is likely. To work without any sense of play, which a lot of people do, is depleting. This play can only occur when people are inspired and creative, love the work they do, or love the people they work with.

Fisher King depressions are often masked. Hardworking, nose-to-the-grindstone people may not even be aware of feeling depressed. They may complain of fatigue, may take antacids or aspirin regularly, may drink too much, smoke too much, eat too much, or watch too much television. Others may find them irritable and no fun to be with. Their work suffers from lack of inspiration and diminished drive. Youthfulness, flexibility, playfulness, and laughter are missing, as is a sense of meaningfulness and creativity. There is no heart in what they do. Life-threatening illnesses, especially heart attacks in men, can be both physical expressions and metaphors for what ails them. Underlying whatever physical form a disease process may take, there is deep disappointment, a lifetime of repressed grief and anger; and the heart hurts from it.

When anger lies just below the surface of a man in authority, he is feared. People keep their distance and do not risk telling him the truth about what they perceive or how they feel, which isolates him further. A king surrounded by courtiers is a man in authority surrounded by codependents; all of which contributes to Fisher King depressions.

STONE MOTHER DEPRESSIONS

Women and men who have devoted their energies to nurturing others and feel that they have been used, or have become depleted or burnt out and are no longer able to care about anyone, are suffering from Stone Mother depressions. Under the depression, they feel angry and deprived. They feel resentful and unrewarded, and they often feel unheard and unrespected as well.

Usually a Stone Mother depression is obvious rather than masked. And more than likely, a woman is the sufferer. She not only knows she's depressed, she also often knows why. It may be because she wanted a child or a relationship that never materialized, or because they now reject her. Or her children or the significant relationships she has, including those with employers and coworkers or clients, take so much from her and return so little. Hidden under her depression and not immediately evident are her anger, grief, and disappointment.

If she has become numb and has "turned to stone," no longer feeling anything for the people she remembers loving, she may feel guilty as well as dead. She needs to be reunited with her own inner young self, who, like Persephone, will bring back spring and with it the return of greenness to the wasteland.

She may suffer from low self-esteem and self-hatred, which are magnified by her use of food, cigarettes, drink, shopping, or television to numb feelings. She is missing youthfulness, playfulness, humor and laughter, creativity, sexuality, and generosity. When the nurturing, good mother archetype that she identified with is gone, people around her are also neglected.

A return or reemergence of the feminine, as Goddess or soul, is the missing element that must come back for the wasteland, the Fisher King, and the Stone Mother to be healed.

Midlife Crisis

Midlife is a time and a state of the psyche. Each of us arrives here sometime during the middle years of adulthood and stays for an indeterminate period of time, as if at a crossroads, before we can go on. It is a time when we passively or actively, consciously or unconsciously, stay on or stray from the course that we earlier embarked upon. What was required of us to get this far, how authentic do we feel, where are we headed? At midlife, we sense that time is passing; we know that this is around the halfway mark and that the rest of life will go by quickly now. We are confronted with the fact that we are aging; we do not have the same body we once had, and much else about us has also changed. A discrepancy may exist between what we have and what we wanted or expected of life, ourselves, or others.

Midlife doldrums, rigid attitudes, addictions, Fisher King and Stone Mother depressions will overtake us if we do not tap into deeper wellsprings in the psyche from which creativity and generativity and meaning can come. The soul requires that we turn inward to individuate. We must go into an inner process, muse, introspect, mull over, hold the dilemmas in consciousness, find our own clarity, tap into what can sustain us spiritually, and act resolutely if it is called for. Whether we repress what is true and suffer the consequences, or act on what we know to be true and discover the price of it, or unconsciously set events in motion that precipitate a crisis, life calls upon us to do inner work. This is a time of adjustment, transition, or crisis that requires us to face change and make choices. The very word *crisis* is derived from the Greek word *krisis*, meaning "decision."

In Chinese, the pictograph for "crisis" is made up of two characters: "danger" and "opportunity." This is especially apparent if it is through falling in love or falling into an enchantment with a person, a new belief, or a project that we are ushered into the crisis. The attraction to a soul mate or to soul work is accompanied by a sense of vitality and youthfulness, which at midlife often serves to animate an interior and relationship wasteland where, for a time, nothing was growing.

The aphrodisiac is usually soul-level conversation; each reveals hopes and vulnerabilities to the other and feels seen, accepted, and touched (always figuratively and often literally) by the other. These are the relationships that invite the neglected, undeveloped, and forgotten parts of ourselves to come forth. Conflicting feelings and allegiances vie for expression, especially if we cannot differentiate our hopes for healing and wholeness from the person who catalyzes the process. We are in great need of clarity at this time, because it is a serious and common mistake to confuse a catalyst with a solution.

Midlife attractions that are used to ward off fears of aging and losing attractiveness, or losing power and potency, are in a different category. They are used much like drugs—as a means of denial or as an equivalent of an antidepressant or an amphetamine high. The soul of the person who serves to make us feel better is immaterial to us. We make no real effort at emotional or spiritual understanding; intimacy is not fostered. In fact, in these relationships, such as they are, depth is actively avoided.

Dream Roles, Personal Roles

Whether we are male or female, all the figures in the Grail legend are within us. We may see ourselves primarily in one role, but a woman may be a wounded Fisher King or a questing knight, and a man may have the role of the Grail Maiden or may be the person through whom the Grail or the Goddess acts to heal wounds and restore the wasteland.

For example, as I was working on this chapter I had a dream in which I had the role of the Fisher King, and a man functioned as the Goddess who healed me. The dream reminded me that the Goddess can work through men as well as women; that whenever healing or divinity is felt in the body, the experience is within the realm of the Goddess.

In the dream, I was in a spacious apartment in a tall building; there were many large rooms filled with small groups of people in conversation. The apartment belonged to a man I had loved in medical school, and there were others there from those years. Somewhere in the apartment we had some privacy and he was cradling my bare body. He put his hand on my left thigh, and I felt a powerful current of electricity and warmth in his touch.

This was a reminder of my own Fisher King wound, for he put his hand at the spot on my thigh where I imagined the Fisher King's was wounded. That it was this particular man who healed me in the dream told me something about the nature of my wound and what needed to be restored in me. The last photograph in *The Family of Man* is of a little boy and a little girl, both about two or three, hand in hand, backs to the camera, walking up a path under sunlit foliage. Years ago, this man and I had seen ourselves in that photograph. For him, in his memory over the years, I was the woman who could play and laugh, whom he would remember in the spring when the daffodils were in bloom. This was the woman I needed to remember myself. She had gone underground as I had become caught up in work, parenting, and partnering, as I felt increasingly unreal and out of touch with my feelings. The Persephone in me who had once gathered flowers in the meadow was repressed in the unconscious, abducted into the underworld.

What I did, men routinely do. They sacrifice the *anima* (the feminine, softer, vulnerable, and emotional aspects of themselves)—usually symbolized by the maiden—in order to be successful in the world, in order to become kings. When being productive and taking care of business is what matters, work occupies mind and time. The daily grind takes its gradual toll, and once spontaneity and emotionality are stifled, the child and maiden archetypes in us are gone, consigned to the underworld. If we lose and do not develop soul connections with people or lose touch with soul-renewing places or activities, we will gradually find that we are inhabiting our own wasteland. If we do not tend to the needs of our souls to be refreshed, and if we do not approach life with an open heart, the wetlands and rainforests of our psyches turn into arid deserts.

ELEVEN

Circumambulation: London

In the midst of my own midlife crisis, I had set out on a real journey to actual places of pilgrimage and in the telling had gotten as far as Glastonbury (four chapters ago). From there, we crossed into the otherworld—to Avalon, the forest, and the wasteland—where the quest for the meaning of the Grail legend had taken me. These places exist in the imaginal world, as well as being my place-names for states of mind and soul.

The journey I am describing moves between outer events and inner reflection, between myth and interpretation—confounding any insistence that the narrative have the directional clarity of a map. The recounting of this pilgrimage follows a circumambulatory course. The pilgrimage itself, however, followed an itinerary. After Glastonbury, the next stop was London.

"Circumambulating" was how C. G. Jung described our experience of the Self, the archetype of meaning that is more than the ego can fully grasp. I think of *Self* as a generic word for God, Goddess, Tao, Higher Power, Spirit, Essence. When life has meaning, it is because we "circle around" this divine, ineffable source and are warmed and illuminated by it. Divinity is more than we can know with our intellect; it is the soul that responds to and recognizes the sacredness of moments when we are in the presence of divinity, love, beauty, wisdom, and truth.

"Circumambulation" is also a fancy way of describing how we "go around in circles"; we may think we travel a straight line from birth to death, but when we realize that we repeatedly encounter circumstances that are our particular lessons, we gain an awareness that the journey is not linear. We spiral through time.

While *circumambulation* literally means "walking around," it has a ritual connotation. When Buddhist and Hindu pilgrims circumambulate Mount Kailas, their holy mountain, they completely circle the base of the mountain as a spiritual act. On my pilgrimage, I was circumambulating sacred sites in many different ways, from literally walking around the Glastonbury Tor to noticing the circumambulatory pattern of my thoughts.

Circumambulating London and Calcutta

In London, Mrs. Detiger introduced me to many different people who were involved in a variety of medical, religious, and peace endeavors. I lectured on "Goddesses in Everywoman" at the English-Speaking Union to a diverse and accomplished group of women for whom spirituality was somehow an essential element in their lives. All of them were active in their various worlds, and this lecture would serve to introduce them to one another. As it turns out, it sparked the beginning of a women's spirituality network in England.

Less than an hour after the lecture, I was in the library of Lambeth Palace at a gathering to celebrate the fiftieth anniversary of the World Council of Faiths. Lambeth Palace is the residence of the archbishop of Canterbury and its library the home of the original Geoffrey of Monmouth manuscript (*Historia Regum Britanniae*, c. 1136) that began the Arthurian literary phenomenon. Geoffrey tells us that he is writing a history of the Britons in which Arthur is presented as a historical figure of mythical dimensions rather than a legendary character. The Grail stories were placed in an Arthurian context because of this manuscript. Had I been on a literary pilgrimage seeking the origins of the Grail as a story, this library would have been a major site on the itinerary; as it was, this connection was one more coincidence on my synchronistic journey. At this gathering, Mrs. Detiger was recognized and thanked for her behind-the-scenes work, which caught her unaware and unprepared to say a few words. It gave me a small glimpse into what she does.

In his talk, Robert Runcie, the archbishop of Canterbury, extended the concept of ecumenicalism to embrace Eastern religions. A number of religious leaders, including Runcie, spoke about how spending time in India had changed them personally.

Each man who spoke about India told a small story that gave us a glimpse of the personal impact the country had had on the young man he had been. I got the impression that religion had become richer, more complex, and more mysterious for them in India, that while they had stayed Christian or Jewish, their experience with Mother India had let something "other" into their psyches, which for monotheistic clergy is the rich diverse pantheism that honors the animistic and earth qualities of the feminine. There is something about India that is atmospherically thicker and heavier and foreign to the male and rational European mentality, which E.M. Forster's *A Passage to India* vividly conveys; several years later I would experience it firsthand in my own travels to India.

I have written books about mythological Greek divinities. The images we have of them are white marble sculptures that invite us to contemplate their Olympian perfection and form. Before I went to India, I thought about the gods and goddessses of other cultures in much the same way. Specifically, before I went to India, I had an idea of the Hindu goddess Kali. She existed in my mind as a missing archetype in Western mythology. There is no equivalent to Kali in the Greek pantheon. She is fierce and frightening, undominated. When women feel their gorge rise with rage, and devouring or trampling their enemies underfoot is an appealing idea, they have no Greek goddess archetype with which to identify. Only Kali has such intensity and power.

However, when I went to the Temple of Kali in Calcutta and saw blood on the ground from the goat that was sacrificed that morning and walked around the temple (which was closed to tourists), it was evident to me that Kali has a visceral reality, as far removed as can be from the cool white smooth marble statues of the Greek divinities in the museums. Blood sacrifice occurs daily and probably has for centuries, and in the midst of the heat and ripe stench, I imagined that human blood was not unknown. Prayer offerings to Kali for fertility were tied to the branches of the temple trees and bushes, left there by women who appeal to Kali to become pregnant. The realm of life and death, fertility and decay, are not abstractions here. There is something distinctly real about Kali as a presence in Calcutta, her namesake city, where everything is more colorful and intense. The crowds themselves as well as myriad impressions—visual, auditory, olfactory, tactile—crowd our senses. Like the city itself, Kali is not so much an object of contemplation as a force to be reckoned with, much like Mother Nature, as cruel as she can be kind.

India as an Initiation

It would seem to me that European men who go to India have an opportunity to disabuse themselves of the notion that they have dominion over Nature. Here they can begin to see that losing patriarchal illusions about superiority and control is the beginning of feminine wisdom. Visiting India can be a humbling experience, requiring one to surrender and adapt to the inevitable. Perhaps for some men, the encounter with India teaches vulnerability, discomfort, humility, and the acceptance that there is a rich material reality beyond their control, which women learn from menstruation, childbirth, and menopause.

As I muse upon the openness to all faiths displayed by these clergymen at Lambeth Palace who spoke about their experience of India, I wonder how much India's pantheism contributes to an acceptance of feminine divinity and how encountering teeming life, decay, and death functions as an initiation into the cycle of life or the Great Mother from whom all life comes and to whom all life returns.

Imagination taps into the collective unconscious, activating images and feelings that we may not know from our own lives, in the same way that the vividness of an encounter with a foreign realm seems to awaken what we intuitively know from collective human experience rather than our own individual lives. This level of awareness comes through the soul. When the Roman poet Terence wrote "Nothing human is foreign to me," he was speaking about soul knowledge, through which we can deeply understand another person's experience or recognize as true something that is beyond what we could know by any other means.

For example, while part of me recoiled from the temple of Kali because it was too much, too visceral and uncomfortable for me, another deeper layer was touched by it. My soul was engaged in an effort to integrate the experience, and so I found myself circumambulating around it, using the psychoanalytic tool of paying attention to my associations, which led me to remembering images that came to my mind when I read *Till We Have Faces,* C.S. Lewis's novel based upon the Psyche myth. I saw a place of worship of the ancient Goddess, a cave back in the hills, where women would go with their grief and rage and guilt and shame, their petitions and prayers, to sit through the night in the darkness of the cave with their dark emotions. In the morning, they would leave comforted and at peace, after pouring out their feelings and blood from a sacrificial bird or animal onto the great dark rock that was the Goddess. This rock endures, accepts, witnesses. Nothing is too much or too terrible to leave with her. The cave is the tomb and womb of the Great Mother, a place of death and new birth, the cauldron of regeneration and transformation; here is another version of the Goddess and the Grail.

The contrast between an air-conditioned museum housing alabaster white statues of deities and the temple of Kali was roughly the distance I had to bridge between an intellectual concept and the visceral reality of Kali, which took more than a visit to Calcutta and a recollection of a novel to do, though both helped. Until I became an initiate into women's mysteries, I could not conceive of divinity as female or sacred revelations in the midst of bodily experience, even when I was presiding, unaware, as priestess to the Goddess in county hospital settings; I was then a physician in training, who recognized dimly that there was something special about delivering babies, and something about being called to sign death certificates in the middle of the night when I was on call for this. Delivery and death are not pretty sights and yet, like the temple of Kali, for all its visceralness, the momentousness or numinosity of birth and death is awesome. A baby often comes out between the legs of a straining mother, along with her feces, with amniotic fluid and blood; sometimes the newborn is covered with greenish-brownish meconium, from its own intrauterine bowel movement, and yet in all of this, if one is a participant and feels how privileged one is to be there when new life emerges, takes a first breath, and cries, it is a moment of great beauty—for all its "yuk." The earthiness of birth and death is the realm of Kali. This is her name in Calcutta, now. But the Goddess has been known by many names, just as she also has been anonymous, the divine matrix whether recognized or named, or not.

A Visit to Dadi Janki

Mrs. Detiger had one more person for me to meet in London before we departed for the next destination: she was a woman from India named Dadi Janki, an unheralded spiritual leader of the Brahma Kumaris, an honored and influential yet little-known worldwide religious organization centered at Mount Abu in northern India. The "BK's" were the inspiration and organization behind an international meditation effort, "A Million Minutes for Peace," and the recipients of the United Nations Peace Messenger Award. We met Dadi Janki at the Brahma Kumaris center, which was in an ordinary house on a residential street in London. I had never heard of her and had no expectations about her or our meeting.

She wore a white cardigan sweater over a simple white Indian sari. She was shorter than I by several inches, which made quite an impression on me since, at just five feet, I hardly ever meet anyone shorter who is not a child. Her face was round, and she had a wonderful smile; she was a sort of combination of cherub and old woman, which made her seem ageless. We met her in an upstairs sitting room. She was accompanied by Sister Jayanti, who occasionally translated for her, but mostly Dadi Janki was easily understood. It seemed to me that words were not her medium anyway. It was her presence that mattered, not how she looked nor what she had to say. She greeted us with the Brahma Kumaris salutation, "Om shanti," which like "Aloha" or "Shalom" was hello, good-bye, and more. "Om shanti" means "I am peace," and this is what she emanated—this and a deeply joyful spirit.

I would meet Dadi Janki two years later in India and again be struck by the combination of joy and wisdom that I felt emanating from her being, as it does from the

Dalai Lama. There is a combination of glowing unselfconscious child and wiseperson in both of them. They are in
the real world committed to a life of service and are sustained by the reality of their spiritual world. They have the
secret of joy. The archetypes they personify are universal,
and if we are receptive to these archetypes in ourselves,
there is a corresponding resonance in us. There is a sympa-
thetic reverberation of inner chords, like that between two
harps: if a harp string is plucked in a room where there is
another harp, the same note string will vibrate in the second harp. Joyfulness is similarly contagious between souls,
if we become attuned to this particular note. That part of
me was growing on this pilgrimage. Two years later in
India, I was aware that being around Dadi Janki had the
effect of constellating the happy-for-no-particular-reason
feelings that a bubbling child just has. So I asked her how
to change the salutation from "Om shanti" ("I am peace")
to "I am joy." It was "Om kushi."

The Dalai Lama and Dadi Janki were themselves
among the "sacred sites" of the pilgrimage. The idea of pilgrimage is to visit sacred sites, places where divinity dwells,
in order to quicken or activate divinity within the pilgrim.
These two have a similar activating effect on people because the archetypal joyful child and spiritual teacher are
imbued with the Self. The divine child aspect within them
was striking to me because this was a part of me that did
need to come back to life again. That child in me felt cherished, looked after, mothered by Mrs. Detiger; as her guid-

ing hand took me in hand on this pilgrimage, my psyche was very receptive to the divine child in others as a result.

Web of Lights

In London I had a growing sense that I was being introduced to people who, in doing whatever it was they did, were part of something much larger. I saw them as bright lights in a vast interconnecting web. This image is archetypal—one that arises from within as an "original idea" in many people, as it had in me.

I have often felt myself to be a point of light, connected to everyone I have ever loved or mattered to, each also being a point of light, in turn connected to those they love, so that somehow we are all part of a vast web of twinkling lights. I think that each individual light can grow brighter or dimmer over the course of a lifetime, and that whenever a light goes out on this web, it affects me. It feels as if everyone who acts compassionately, works to raise consciousness, to save the planet, to make a difference in some significant way is linked to everyone else who also does.

This image of the web of lights came to me many years ago, when a former patient of mine who had moved across the continent wrote that she had not been able to commit suicide after all. In a period of despair, she had finally decided to exercise "this option" that she had talked about for so long, only to find that she could not do it. When I heard from her, I was greatly relieved that she was alive.

And I knew that even if I never heard from her or saw her again, she and I were connected. The image that came to mind with this realization was of a web of lights; when I thought of her as dead, I saw and felt a light at the end of a long strand that connected us go out. There would be darkness where she once was, and it mattered that she was alive.

In Europe, my sense of the size of that web grew enormously. I was touching in with those people whose strands reached around the world, and I felt that I was plugging my American web of lights into a great network.

Lights in the Darkness

I thought of the day I had spent being a tourist in Amsterdam before leaving for Glastonbury. I now realize that it was part of the pilgrimage, too. I had visited the Anne Frank Haus, climbing the steep narrow stairs to the back of the house, where she, her parents, and others were hidden from the Nazis during the occupation of Holland. In what is now a museum, I read each panel, looked at each photograph, and tried to feel what it must have been like to be her.

I felt a wave of gratitude for the many ordinary Dutch citizens who sheltered Jewish people at risk of their own lives. I also felt a sense of kinship with Anne. During those same wartime years, I had been a child, too. As a Japanese American living in California, whose family had managed to escape being in a concentration camp, I had felt only a fraction of the apprehension of attracting hostile attention that Anne Frank and her family must have felt. We didn't have to go into hiding, but we did have to move often during the evacuation and relocation of everyone of Japanese ancestry, initially staying just one step ahead of martial law. During the war years, I went to seven elementary schools in five states. I had to enter new situations repeatedly. Since the United States was at war with Japan, and I was ethnically pure Japanese, each time there was a possibility that I would encounter hostility. My grandparents on both sides had immigrated from Japan, and though both of my parents were born in this country, had we not gotten out of California, we would have all been incarcerated in the concentration camps.

Being in the Anne Frank Haus made an emotional impression on me that increased the impact of what she wrote. As I read the entries from *Anne Frank: The Diary of a Young Girl* that are a prominent part of the exhibit and looked at the other information and photographs, the enormity of the Darkness and the brightness of her light and her innocence moved me to tears.

On July 15, 1944, she wrote in her diary, ". . . in spite of everything I still believe that people are good at heart." By then she and the others had been in hiding from the Nazis for over two years. On August 4, 1944, they were arrested. In March 1945, Anne died in the concentration camp at Bergen-Belsen. She was fifteen.

Anne Frank lived and died in a historical period in which lights were going out all over Europe, literally and metaphorically. She had been a bright light in a darkening web. Her light did not go out when she died, however. Instead, through her words she inspired and continues to inspire; her light grows brighter.

Had my patient been able to kill herself, I sense that the light that linked her to me would have gone out. Not just because she died, but because it would have meant that the light in *her* had gone out, and death by suicide would have been the outer expression of what had already happened to her soul.

Each person who follows his or her own light is a light in the web. When what we do grows out of inner conviction that whatever it may be that we choose to do in a moment or in our lifetime is meaningful, there is soul in the choice. Who we are inside needs to find authentic expression in how we live. The love we feel for what we do brings us joy. The belief in the capacity of the human heart to love in spite of the expressions of despair and hatred that we see happening keeps that light glowing. It has to do with keeping faith; to believe that we matter and can make a difference, or even act as if this were so until it becomes an inner conviction. The child and the wiseperson are the light-bearers in the psyche who need to prevail over the fear of appearing naive and/or foolish, which the mind may counsel. Within ourselves and in the world, there are cynical forces that try to snuff out the lights—to make us distrust our intuition, devalue the wellspring of perennial wisdom that the soul otherwise naturally drinks from, and in fear choose power over love.

TWELVE

The Greening of the Wasteland: Findhorn

We boarded the night train from London to Inverness, Scotland, for the next part of the pilgrimage. Now we were four: Elinore Detiger, Soozi Holbeche, Freya Reeves, and me. Until now, I had been thinking of Elinore as "Guiding Hand," because her fine hand had been shaping my experience on this trip so far. Now she became a sister pilgrim, too.

We were on our way north to Findhorn. Findhorn is a New Age community near one of the northernmost coasts of Scotland. In my mind, it was an Eden, a mythological destination like the Garden of the Hesperides where the tree with golden apples grew. Findhorn had gotten worldwide attention in the 1970s as a magical place where people communed with plants and grew vegetables and fruits of remarkable size and variety in the worst possible soil conditions.

We caught "the sleeper" at Euston Station in London; well named, for sleep came easily with the clickity-clacking lullaby of the moving train. Each of us went into our own little cozy compartment for the night and slept in a pull-down bed that filled the space, almost wall to wall.

Hot tea and a change of scenery greeted us the next morning. The countryside outside the train window was familiar for the first time since I had arrived in Europe. This was Scotland, but it looked just like western Marin County in northern California in the winter months. Overnight, the lush green gentle hills of England had been replaced by rougher terrain. The hills were craggy and rock-strewn, beautiful and bleak at the same time. It was chilly. As we traveled north, the early summer air was no more; it felt like winter was barely past.

A red Peugeot rental car awaited us at the Inverness train station. There was a chill in the air and the skies were gray. Elinore drove, taking us in a northeasterly direction. It was a short drive to our destination. Given my fantasies of an Eden, I never expected Findhorn to look like a trailer camp in the middle of nowhere, which was the first impression I had as we pulled off the highway into the parking area, where the Findhorn gift shop greets the visitor.

Findhorn was founded in the 1960s, when Eileen and Peter Caddy, their three boys, and Dorothy Maclean settled in a trailer near a rubbish dump on the edge of sand dunes and followed the spiritual guidance that directed them to set about creating a small garden in the sand and scrub. Eileen Caddy heard an inner voice that directed them. Dorothy Maclean contacted the archetypal intelligence or *deva* of each plant species to learn what was needed. The devas (a word that stems from a Sanskrit word meaning "shining ones") were described by her as "angels, great Beings whose lives infuse and create all of Nature." Peter's intuition and energy went into the work of manifesting the instructions that the women received. All three felt divinely directed. The results were extraordinary, word spread, and others were drawn there. This was the beginning of a spiritual community whose members saw themselves as participating in a unique experiment in conscious communication and cooperation between humans and Nature. By the early 1970s, it had grown to a community of more than three hundred people.

When we arrived at Findhorn, Peter Caddy had been long gone to California. Eileen Caddy, however, happened to be there; she was touching in on her way to and from other places. We would have tea with her later, in her "caravan" (English for trailer), which was homey. She looked like a solid, respectable, pillar-of-any-community woman who wouldn't appear out of place in the American Midwest. Though she was the psychic whose guidance had led to the founding of Findhorn, there was no airy-fairy hocus-pocus about her. That she would be there during the short time we visited was like the fact that the organist was playing as I entered Chartres Cathedral: it enhanced whatever it was that I had come to learn and felt like synchronicity.

We joined the community at lunch and had organic food in the low-ceilinged dining room filled with tables and benches. The people were of all ages, from children to elders. There were lots of Americans: the first impression was that these people were northern California expatriates, though most were actually Europeans.

The "magic" of Findhorn was not immediately evident to me, even upon seeing the gardens, for a Californian is used to bounty and beauty on a grander scale.

The Findhorn Community had its own equivalent of a cathedral; it was the one imposing building there. In a community of caravans and one-story wooden structures, it is prominent in size and height, made of stone and adorned with art. Like cathedrals of old, which were the center of community life and not just a place of worship, the Universal Hall is used for many purposes and performances. It was built as an expression of faith and love by the people who lived there, directed by visionaries and intuitives who worked together on this project. Symbolic meaning went into its five-sided shape (the number 5 represents perfection, the meeting of spirit and form), sacred geometry guided the proportions, rituals consecrated it, crystals were planted in its foundation, and it was built where ley lines come together. In this hall and in the meditation room (the sanctuary), conscious efforts were directed toward creating sacred spaces, which like pilgrimage sites that "quicken the divinity" would affect the psyches of community members and visitors.

Greening the Wasteland

The gardens of Findhorn were so much less grand than I had expected that initially I was not impressed. Wonder at what was accomplished came when I contrasted the thriving gardens with the barrenness of the area, and when I saw the indigenous gravel and sand soil and realized how chilly it was even this late in May. While Findhorn is at sea level, it is so far north that the land and the weather resemble terrain above the timberline. Seen in this perspective, their vegetable gardens, fruit-bearing trees, and beautiful flowers are like an oasis in the desert—only this was a garden that existed because its founders had tapped into a spiritual source and found a spring of information and wisdom.

Women were the mediums through whom the vision came and the devas communicated. In communicating with the devas of the plants, Dorothy Maclean, especially, brought the wisdom of Nature to the community. As on Avalon, Mother Earth, the Goddess, Great Mother communicated through women and to them; and as the medium through which feminine divinity as Mother Nature came, these contemporary women functioned as priestesses of the Goddess. The wisdom that came through them turned a wasteland green.

At Findhorn, Dorothy Maclean was the bearer of the wisdom that would bring the wasteland to life; as such, she was the Grail Maiden. This Grail literally heals the wasteland and spiritually brings us an experience of the intelligence that is in all living things. This Grail has not come fully into the world; it has been brought into consciousness and worked its healing magic at Findhorn, but its meaning and mystery, reality and potential have not emerged into mainstream consciousness. Everything on this earth, including people, remains exploitable because the wounded king—patriarchal consciousness with its emphasis on power—prevails.

In musing about these remarkable gardens of Findhorn that grow out of a wasteland, I am reminded of how similarly remarkable it is when someone with a bleak and barren childhood, devoid of security and full of abuse, does not respond in kind by becoming a battering, abusive, cynical adult but instead becomes a loving person who can trust others. It's a miracle when someone's life begins as a barren trash heap and ends up a garden. On seeing "the garden" without knowing its history, we miss the meaning and wonder and inspiration that it exists at all, just as I almost did on seeing Findhorn.

I have heard women who survived such childhoods with their souls intact describe how Nature provided them sanctuary. A special tree, foothills to roam in, the sea or the sky, animals or a garden, and an inner world that remained inviolate were soul-saving for them. In the privacy and solitude of their own minds, they could wonder and imagine and hold thoughts and images that were the seeds of later creativity. The spirituality, the wisdom, the connection with Nature that we find in the writings of Alice Walker and Mary Oliver, have much in common with the wisdom of the devas that was given a voice by Dorothy Maclean. When the capacity for Sight is not recognized, might the "overactive imaginations" of many children be communication with this invisible, spiritual realm? Might this communion be the source of their wisdom and spiritual understanding and call to seek refuge in Nature? I not only think so, but I also see that solitude is necessary for this inner secret garden to develop. When a child keeps her inner world to herself, it will not be desecrated; it also may not be remembered later in life unless the child or adult searches for and finds words of her own for it.

Greening Power of the Grail

A rubbish dump on the edge of sand dunes is an ideal site to show how to heal a wasteland. The contrast between the inhospitable terrain where Findhorn began and the resulting gardens demonstrates what can be done when we have access to *viriditas* or *greening power*. At Findhorn, it came through the psyches of women who could cross through the mists into the invisible world of the Goddess and bring this wisdom into a community that valued it. Metaphorically, the greening power is the Grail that can heal the wasteland.

Viriditas or *greening power* are theological terms made up by Hildegard of Bingen (1098–1179). We know of them today through the writings of theologian Matthew Fox. Fox comments that Hildegard used *viriditas* as a synonym of blessing for fruitfulness and creativity. For her, salvation or healing was "the return of greening power and moistness." In the essay "Viriditas: Greening Power" in *Illuminations of Hildegard of Bingen,* Fox writes:

> Hildegard contrasts greening power or wetness with the sin of drying up. A dried-up person and dried-up culture lose their ability to create. This is why drying up is so grave a sin for Hildegard—it interferes with our exalted vocation to create. "Humankind alone is called to co-create," she declares.
>
> Viriditas . . . is God's freshness that humans receive in their spiritual and physical life-forces. It is the power of springtime, a germinating force, a fruitfulness that comes from God and penetrates all creation. This powerful life force is found in the non-human as well as the human realms. "The earth sweats, germinating power from its very pores," she declares.
>
> Instead of seeing body/soul in a warring struggle as did Augustine, Hildegard sees that "the soul is the freshness of the flesh, for the body grows and thrives through it just as the earth becomes fruitful through moisture." Mary, the mother of Jesus, is celebrated for being the

viridissima virga, the greenest of the green branches, the most fruitful of us all. She is a branch "full of the greening power of springtime," and in such a thought, there resound deep overtones of the goddess tradition in religion.

Green and the Grail are related to healing and divinity. In the alchemical texts the *benedicta viriditas* (the blessed green) was a sign of the beginning of the reanimation of the material; it showed that vitality was returning to the process. In *The Grail Legend,* Emma Jung and Marie-Louise von Franz describe the connection between green and the Grail:

> As a color of vegetation and, in a wider sense, of life, green is obviously in harmony with the nature of the Grail. . . . In ecclesiastical symbolism, green is the color of the Holy Ghost (the comforter) or the anima mundi, and in the language of the mystics it is the universal color of divinity.

Recalling the green silk-and-velvet hood that I put on over academic black at my medical school graduation, I am reminded of the connection also between the divinity and healing, which goes back to the Temple of Ascelipius and, before the Greeks, to the Goddess.

Wet and Moist and Green and Juicy

In the Grail legend, the king needs to be healed of his wound in order for green to return to an arid wasteland. He is an old man with a wound in his thigh. The site of his wound suggests that he has lost his connection with sexuality, fertility, generativity, and creativity, and suffers from what Hildegard considered the ultimate sin of drying up or aridness. In her correspondence with archbishops, bishops, abbots, and priests, the Fisher Kings of her times, she urged them to stay "wet and moist and green and juicy" and to let "merciful dew" into the heart to overcome dryness.

To be wet and moist and green and juicy is to be emotionally alive. Our bodies express authentic feelings through moisture: tears of happiness or grief flow, or we laugh so much that our eyes tear up, or our eyes become moist when certain emotions are touched or memories are recalled. In contrast, Fisher King depressions are emotionally arid, dry-eyed, and without moisture.

Think of our own bodies: when we are sexually aroused, our bodies respond with moisture; juices flow in anticipation and desire; ejaculations and secretions are wet. When there is no natural lubrication, there is likely emotional dryness as well.

The fetus grows in amniotic fluid, labor begins in earnest with the breaking of this "bag of waters," and the newborn emerges into the world wet with fluids. Stimulated by the birth and the flow of milk from her breasts, a woman can become a nursing mother, or the milk may dry up.

To sweat doing physically taxing work or to work out until one sweats usually means that this is a real effort. To have sweat break out for other reasons usually means that fear or anxiety is intense.

When we say that something is mouth-watering, we are describing what the body does in anticipation of the pleasure of eating it. These are all ways of being "juicy." All have to do with intensity, involvement, and emotional fluidity; they are body and psyche reactions. To be wet and moist and juicy is to be real; it is how we are when we are genuine, when our bodies and emotions express what we feel.

Hildegard of Bingen said we should be "green" as well. To be green at anything is to be young and inexperienced. In the Old West, a "greenhorn" was such a person. Men are made to feel ashamed of being green at anything, and so cover it up as much as possible. Yet only by being green and innocent, by having or rediscovering a part of ourselves that is green, can we be a Perceval, an innocent fool who can enter the Grail Castle, or be the child who can enter the Kingdom of God or the Garden of the Goddess. Findhorn's gardens grew in the wasteland because people communicated with nature spirits or devas and cooperatively co-created the garden. These people had to trust the children in themselves who believed in this more than they feared "the men in the white coats" or the opinion of more rational minds. There is some twinkly-eyed humor in using the biblical advice "By their fruits, you shall know them" as a measure of the sanity as well as the divinity of Findhorn.

The promise of spring and the return of greenness to the barren land is also a psychological possibility symbolized by the return of the maiden goddess Persephone to her mother, Demeter. Hildegard described Mary as having this Persephone effect upon the psyche when she wrote: "You glowing, most green, verdant sprout . . . you bring lush greenness once more" to the "shrivilled and wilted" of the world. In Egypt, the Mother Goddess is Isis and it is her divine sone Osiris's return from death and dismemberment that is equated with the annual greening of the Nile Valley and a similar symbolic promise. Osiris is the only Egyptian divinity whose face is green. Midlife depressions and creative blocks are over when we become green and juicy. Then life is full of interests and vitality. We are fascinated with the play of ideas, images, and feelings that lead us to being creative, innovative, and inventive. In this spirit and with an open heart, we can love again.

Sister Pilgrims

The company I was in—Elinore, Freya, and Soozi—was as important an ingredient of this part of the journey as were the sites we visited. I had not met any of the others before this pilgrimage, and yet we came together like old friends. The presence of the child archetype in all of us was obvious in the happy sounds we made, in our spontaneity. In a moment of stillness in a sacred place, in the collective impulse to meditate for a moment, in the naturalness of saying something profound, we would find the wisewoman and priestess among us. Perhaps Soozi would initiate a small ritual. Or Freya would say something from her heart. Or Elinore would casually refer to something that was of planetary significance. Or I might see the symbolism of the situation. We laughed more than I had in years, so hard on one stretch of the road that we had to pull over until the paroxysms of laughter had passed. There was enough "mother" to go around without any one of us having to carry the role for anyone else or for the group. We were all independent women and also caretaking women, and among us whatever was called for was done.

This small group of sister pilgrims became the seed experience, the pattern, the morphic field for women's groups, workshops, and pilgrimages that became part of my later work—this and my participation in a women's prayer-meditation group that has met regularly for six years. Here pilgrimage is the metaphor for our lives and the sacred site in which we meet comes into being when we sit together and pray or meditate. To be together in this space nurtures us; it feels as if we generate an inaudible hum in which each woman's psyche contributes to a harmonic that is attuned to the heart. It's comforting, like being with Mother, not personal mother but the mother archetype. In the theology of Protestant Christianity of my experience, the Trinity of Father, Son, and Holy Ghost was male. In my own experience, because Holy Spirit or Holy Ghost was invisible, it became genderless. In the

New Testament, the Holy Spirit descended in the form of a dove, which is a feminine symbol, and was called the Comforter. When we need comforting—when we have been hurt, or are in pain or grief, or are sick and afraid—we feel small and want mother to put her arms around us, to kiss the hurt and make it go away. Even when our own experience of mother was not this, we yearn for what we know is archetypal; we miss Mother.

Watching wild doves come among raucous blue jays to eat birdseed on my deck at home, I intuitively felt why the dove is a symbol of peace and divinity. There is something in its aura that makes a dove very different from a pigeon, which it superficially resembles. Whatever that something is, the blue jays respect. I was surprised to see them become quieter and make room for the dove as if the dove were an invited guest, when the approach of any other bird increased their competitiveness and noise level. Doves also have a feminine grace and bearing. Long before Christianity, the dove was the goddess Aphrodite's symbol. Hidden in the symbology of the male Holy Spirit is the presence of the goddess of love and Beauty who was also a mother goddess.

A group of women can constellate a Mother morphic field when we gather together in a sacred circle. We create a *temenos,* which means "sanctuary" in Greek. In a women's circle, every woman in the circle is herself and an aspect of every other woman there as well. There is no vertical hierarchy in a circle, and when a circle is a temenos, it is a safe place to tell the truth of our own feelings, perceptions, and experiences. Recovery groups based on Alcoholics Anonymous recreate the temenos at every meeting in a similar way.

For a women's circle to work as a spiritual and psychological cauldron for change and growth, we need to see every woman in the circle as a sister who mirrors back to us reflections of ourselves. This means that whatever happened to her could have happened to us, that whatever she has felt or done is a possibility for us, that she is someone toward whom we feel neither superior nor inferior nor indifferent. These are not just concepts but the emotional reality that comes from listening to women tell the truth about their lives. Additional depth comes from the psychological awareness that strong reactions to another woman may occur because she represents something in ourselves that is psychologically charged; our reactions are not just about her but about us. Perhaps we can't stand her because she expresses experiences we have repressed; maybe we find her difficult because we react to her like we did to our personal mother or some other significant figure; maybe we are drawn to her because she embodies a potential in ourselves and the positive qualities we so admire in her are growing in us; maybe we avoid her because we fear our own addictions, dependency, or neediness. In this way, we are symbolic figures for each other that we need to understand as we would symbols in a personal dream.

I also had the feeling that by being together on this pilgrimage, we women—with that permeability of ego structure that male psychology has been so critical of—absorbed the essence of who we were with each other. Of course we talked, but there was no way we could have pooled our collective experience, values, and wisdom—and yet, I think in some measure we did.

I wonder, for example, how much of the meaning of Findhorn came to me because I was with Soozi and Elinore, even though there was surprisingly little talk about it. Soozi had once lived at Findhorn and had taken Findhorn out into the world, doing workshops in Africa, Australia, the United States, and Europe, so her ties were deep. It wasn't clear about Elinore's relationship to Findhorn but she too seemed to have a significant connection with the vision and the work of Findhorn.

On this journey, I found—as pilgrims have always known—that going to sacred places affects the psyche of the pilgrim. I came back sensing that my psyche had also been affected in this nonverbal, deepening way by contact with the people I met and my sister pilgrims. I was reminded of my friend Brooke Medicine Eagle, who has a crystal that touched the great Hopi crystal, and who in turn touched this crystal to one of mine in the belief that the collective spiritual wisdom of the Hopi nation is transmitted by contact from one crystal to the next. Besides wondering if this could be true, I wonder if people might be able to transfer or transmit impressions, as crystals are reputed to do.

This speculation came from sensing that something like this was happening with my sister pilgrims, and from meeting Dadi Janki and the Dalai Lama. I was affected by being in their presence and recalled a conversation I had had with William Tiller years ago. Bill was a professor at Stanford in one of the "hard" sciences. His wife Jean was psychic, which led him into the avocation of parapsychology. We talked about Jesus, and Jung's concept of the "constellating" effect people have on each other. In Arthur Koestler's book *The Robot and the Lotus,* Koestler described how an enormous crowd of people in India would gather in a field to hear a guru, who would be but a small speck they could see from a distance. Without a sound system, the guru would say something that only the people immediately around him could hear, and yet the people who came felt spiritually affected.

The guru had an effect on their psyches. In Jungian language, he "constellated the Self" in them. Might this also be one explanation for the effect Jesus had when he preached—that the baptism by the Holy Spirit that initiated his ministry, infused him with divinity that could awaken latent divinity in others? *Infuse, constellate, quicken, incarnate* are for me words that attempt to express the same meaning.

The Green Magic of Findhorn and the Network of Light

Findhorn captures the imagination because it is a place where parables and metaphors that have existed in the invisible world of collective human imagination have become real. Where once there was literally a trash heap and soil too poor and sandy to grow anything in, a garden grew; and thus the idea of the wasteland becoming green again really happened in this small place. Findhorn is more than an accomplishment or a successful experiment; it spurs the imagination and serves as a source of inspiration about what might be possible. We could heal the earth and bring forth abundance.

Tingles go up the spine when a personally held myth is revealed to be a shared one, when we realize that something we imagined might actually be happening. For me, it was not the garden at Findhorn that sent the tingles but hearing about "the network of Light." In *Faces of Findhorn*, Peter Caddy tells of meeting a woman he refers to only as Naomi in the Philippines, who told him of "the network of Light." "She was the focal point for a group whose work had been to locate centers of Light throughout the world and to link them telepathically." Later she came to Findhorn and became one of the founders. Twice a day for three or four years, a group at Findhorn met to meditate and communicate telepathically with these centers. They did this believing that these invisible strands were strengthened in this way with the numerous centers in this network of light.

As I could see on this pilgrimage and appreciate even more on my return, sacred places are being resanctified all over the earth, and people are also finding the sacred within themselves. Every sacred place and every sacred person is indeed like a point of light in a great web whose strands grow brighter each time a pilgrim travels from one place or person to another. The light grows brighter each time any one of us recognizes that there is something truly divine and of the Goddess in herself or himself, something that is inseparable from others and from Nature.

THIRTEEN

Musings: Iona and Other Sacred Places

F rom Findhorn, we went to
several nearby sites, to the Clava Cairns, Pluscarden Abbey,
and Cluny Hill—places that I had never heard of before
and about which I had absolutely no expectations. As we
set out on that particular day, I felt more like a tourist than
a pilgrim. I could not have guessed that I would so tangi-
bly feel the presence and power of an energy source at the
Clava Cairns and Pluscarden, and that of all the places of

pilgrimage, Elinore would be most moved by what she experienced at Cluny Hill, where I would feel nothing at all.

Michael Lindfield was our guide to the Clava Cairns. Michael had been at Findhorn for a decade, during which time he had been a major "light," and now he and his family were packing to leave for Seattle to join David Spangler, Dorothy Maclean, and others from Findhorn who were settling in the Pacific Northwest. He was a peaceful, strong, quiet, tall, gentle presence; I think of him as one of those sacred people, a crystal I touched in with who, along with the sacred places, made the pilgrimage what it was.

The Clava Cairns

The Clava Cairns are within a half hour of Findhorn on a back road. Here, in a site that seems undisturbed by history or tourists, are stones that have been in this place for four or five thousand years.

We approached the first of the three cairns from the rear. The cairns are in a green grassy-mossy clearing surrounded by a rim of tall trees. From behind, the first cairn appears to be a large, rounded mound of stones, covering about as much ground as a house and reaching to where the eaves of a single-story house might be. Boulder-sized stones surround the periphery, within which are piled smoothed stones that look like those found in a riverbed. At the front of the cairn, also outlined by larger boulders, is a passageway that leads into a round space in its center.

The walls of the passageway and the center are perpendicular, made so by layers of carefully selected rock. From the inside, looking down the passage out, one sees large gateway stones with spiral markings in small rounded indentations.

This is a vaginal passageway into a womb space. Once in the center, all of us could feel a concentration of energy and sense that there was something feminine about it, as ephemeral as such a perception is. Once again I felt like I was a tuning fork and on a cellular level my body was responding to strong vibrations or emanations. I sensed that I was in an invisible, highly charged energy field. Later, after the others moved on, I returned to this cairn to reexperience this new way of perception that I had first felt in the center of my chest at Chartres Cathedral.

I thought of the labyrinth on the floor of Chartres Cathedral, which is located where the womb would be on a body the size of the church if its arms were outstretched at the transepts; and then of the uterine-shaped Glastonbury Tor, which may be a three-dimensional equivalent of the two-dimensional labyrinth, where I had felt, as so many do, that there must be a hollow chamber in the Tor and a passageway in. And now, unexpectedly, here at the Clava Cairns, I was inside a structure that felt like a representation of the womb of the Goddess.

It reminded me of American Indian kivas, rounded structures that are partially under the earth and that served as incubating and initiating chambers for young men.

They would enter as boys and emerge from this womb space as men. Each was twice born; first from his mother's body and then from the kiva. The archetype of initiation is a transformation; the initiate dies to his old life and is born into his new identity.

I wondered what took place in this cairn. Was this, too, a rebirthing place—was it both tomb and womb? I could readily imagine how powerful it would be to enter the cairn in the dark. While it now is open to the sky, might it originally have been covered?

The cairn has a circle of standing stones around it. After spending time in the center of the cairn, feeling the energy of the place and being affected by it, I next was moved to pay my respects to each standing stone, each of which felt like a stone equivalent of an "old soul."

The second cairn is smaller and in the shape of an un-broken oval, like a doughnut with a center space. We referred to it as the egg. The only way in is over the stones. The structure is smaller and lower in height than the first cairn. I felt like lying down in it, which I did. There is something compelling about lying directly on the earth, which children naturally do, fully spread out. I recall that I used to occasionally climb a small hill near my house when I was a preadolescent, flatten out the tall weeds and lie down on them where I would be hidden from view, and be content. On this pilgrimage I had become aware of Earth energies; might children who lie directly on the Earth in solitude and sanctuary be looking to be held by the Great Mother? Alice Walker, who has always been nourished by nature, often lies directly on the Earth. I have heard her say, "The Earth is the only Goddess I need."

The third cairn is shaped like the first, with a passage like a birth canal into its hollow center, only it is taller and the energy is different, more active and stirring. Around it also are standing stones, with one a particularly striking, tall, rectangular monument stone.

It awed me to realize that these stones that are not even mortared had been here for four to five thousand years. It awed me that when I stood in the center of the first cairn, I felt the same energy that I had experienced in the transept at Chartres Cathedral. I felt that same warmth and pressure and something akin to vibration in the center of my chest, where the energies of the heart concentrate. Heart and womb images kept coming to me on this pilgrimage as expressions of the Goddess and the Grail; they were forms of thought that came out of the sensations in my own body. It is a different way of perceiving and knowing, an embodied consciousness unlike the mental grasp of a subject that I got through my education and medical training.

Pluscarden Abbey

We drove from the Clava Cairns and did some sightseeing on the way to Pluscarden Abbey, stopping at Randolph's Leap to gaze down upon rushing rivers of dark water, stained black by coursing through peat. From the color, they could have been tributaries of the mythical underground river Styx. Pluscarden Abbey is also not far from

Findhorn. It's in an exceedingly peaceful setting, tucked away and reached by tree-lined back roads. It is an imposing stone church that looks like it could grace a college campus in the United States, appearing as it does to be relatively young in age, well maintained, and in use.

In it is a Mary Chapel used exclusively by the brothers who live and work at the abbey. Visitors do not enter it. A window is cut into the wall between the main church and the chapel, allowing a view of its altar.

Standing at this window, I had the most remarkable experience. The energy that I had felt in sacred places was more intense here than in any other place we'd been on this pilgrimage. Along the way, I had been irreverently saying that the air molecules are "fatter" in sacred places, because the air in these places feels charged in a palpable way. And now I felt bathed in a stream of energy from the Mary Chapel. It felt like molecules were moving in a current that rushed over me, swirled around me, and blessed me.

With my Protestant background, Mary is as foreign to me as the idea of worshiping a Goddess. But this experience at Pluscarden, and the historical awareness I'd gained on this pilgrimage that places sacred to the Goddess were either made into Mary chapels (or cathedrals) or had Saint Michael's abbeys built over them, certainly made me think about the connection between the Goddess and the Virgin Mary.

At the end of *The Mists of Avalon,* an aging Morgaine, the last priestess of the Goddess, crosses from Avalon to Glastonbury and enters a Mary Chapel, where she realizes for the first time that the Goddess will continue to be in the world even if Christianity triumphs. Marion Zimmer Bradley's fictionalized account parallels my own remarkable experience at Pluscarden.

> Morgaine followed the young girl into the small side chapel. There were flowers here, armfuls of apple blossoms, before a statue of a veiled woman crowned with a halo of light; and in her arms she bore a child. Morgaine drew a shaking breath and bowed before the Goddess.
>
> The girl said, "Here we have the Mother of Christ, Mary the Sinless. God is so great and terrible I am always afraid before his altar, but here in the chapel of Mary, we who are her avowed virgins may come to her as our Mother, too. . . . And here is a very old statue that our bishop gave us, from his native country . . . one of their saints, her name is Brigid. . . . "
>
> Morgaine looked on the statue of Brigid, and she could feel the power coming from it in great waves that permeated the chapel. She bowed her head.
>
> But Brigid is not a Christian saint, she thought, even if Patricius thinks so. That is the Goddess as she is worshipped in Ireland. And I know it, and even if they think otherwise, these women know the power of the Immortal. Exile her as they may, she will prevail. The Goddess will never withdraw herself from mankind.

Cluny Hill

After Pluscarden we drove to Cluny Hill. The sacred site is the hill itself, which is located behind the building they call Cluny Hill, Findhorn's Guest and Conference Center.

It is located some miles from Findhorn itself. Cluny Hill is considered a major power point in the area, a place where ley lines converge. There is also a legend that Jesus came to Britain as a young boy with his uncle Joseph of Arimathea and visited Cluny Hill and Glastonbury.

It's a small hill with a single-file path through the underbrush and trees that spirals up to a small clearing at the top and then spirals down. The four of us took this path, with Elinore bringing up the rear and me leading the way. She and Freya felt as if they were entering an ancient place. And Elinore had a powerful visual impression besides: she saw us become robed and hooded figures, the ancients who walked this path before. For her, Cluny Hill was the site of the most sacred moment of the pilgrimage; she entered another time and was awed by the experience of being there. The transient and powerful experience of being in the same place but in another time (as if in an earlier lifetime) was intensified because in it she was a participant in a sacred procession.

In contrast, I was unimpressed. There was nothing remarkable at all about Cluny Hill for me. It had been a lighthearted excursion. Someday I would like to go back to Cluny Hill to see, as I expect, what I missed. After all, the experience of any sacred site depends upon the interaction between the place and the visitor's psyche. I suspect that leading the way through the woods and up the path, I was more a girl scout than a pilgrim. Plus I was still full from the experiences at Pluscarden and the Clava Cairns.

Iona

We left Findhorn and began making our way toward Iona. Our route took us past Loch Ness, across northern Scotland, and westward to the coast. At Oban, we caught a ship-sized ferry to the island of Mull. Then we drove across the length of Mull to take a small passengers-only ferry to Iona. It requires considerable effort and coordination of ferry boat schedules to make it to the very small island of Iona. For all the difficulty in getting to this remote place, it has for centuries been on the beaten path for pilgrims. The Scots say: "When Edinburgh was a rock and Oxford was a swamp, Iona was famous."

Iona is one of the smaller islands of the Inner Hebrides, off the western coast of Scotland. It is a simple and serene island only three and a half miles long. And like Glastonbury, Iona is thought to be a place where the veil between mundane and divine worlds is thinner. It is an island made of ancient rock, geologically different from its neighbors. And it is a source of Iona marble, a beautiful white marble with streaks of soft celadon green.

Iona has been called the cradle of Christianity, for it was from Iona that Saint Columba brought the Christian faith—as Celtic Christianity—to Scotland, the north of England, and northern Europe in the sixth century. Its monastery was a famous center of learning and art. Here, an illuminated manuscript that became the Book of Kells is believed to have originated. Over the centuries Celtic

Christianity came under the influence of mainstream Christianity, and in the thirteenth century the Benedictines built a beautiful abbey on Iona. This abbey was restored in the twentieth century by the Protestant Church of Scotland and is now the home of the Iona Community, an ecumenical Christian community.

We stepped off the ferry onto the beach and into tranquil time. Sea and sky, stone buildings and stone hillsides, sturdy people and sturdy plant life live together in an ever-changing climate that can be gentle or fierce. We needed to dress warmly, even though it was late May. Our pace was set by Mother Nature and the services at the abbey. We stayed at a homey, simple hotel, each in a room that in its simplicity and size could have been in a monastery.

It was a perfect place for retreat and reflection. My dream life became very active while we were there. On the High Altar at Glastonbury I had participated in a personal ritual in which I had brought the five significant people in my life into my mind and heart, and asked them to forgive me. Now my dreams were in the spirit of that ritual; in one series of dreams my husband appeared and acknowledged our separation. I felt only sadness and compassion; healing was taking place in me.

Iona was both a pilgrimage site and a time out (or time *in*). What had begun at Glastonbury as the *vesica piscis* experience—in which I felt the mutual presence of God the Father and the Mother Goddess and experienced myself as a chalice in which both came together in my heart center—came back to me at Iona. Now on Iona, I found a symbol that united the Father and the Mother. On the abbey grounds, there is a tall Celtic cross at least nine hundred years old. A ring, which is a symbol of the Goddess, is incorporated into this cross; it encircles where the two arms of the cross intersect. Unlike Roman and Protestant Christianity, Celtic Christianity retained a belief in the sacredness of the physical world; instead of driving out the Goddess it incorporated her and kept faith with its pagan and mystical roots.

The Celtic crosses, the rebuilt abbey, and the stone chapel, in which I read T. S. Eliot's "Burnt Norton" from *Four Quartets* to my sister pilgrims, are all physical witnesses and carriers of tradition and history, around which there is a sense of sacred place. Iona is also renowned as a source place of mysticism, which is why it is described as a place where the veil is thinner. The veil is a barrier between this world and the otherworld; the mystic pierces the veil.

The Woman in the Heart of Women

Iona is linked with the mystical writing of Fiona MacLeod. Elinore took us into a small bookstore on Iona and told us about Fiona MacLeod. When she had first come to Iona years before, she had found several of MacLeod's books among the used books there. MacLeod was the female personality who lived inside a man named William Sharp (1855–1905). Psychologically, we might define Fiona as William Sharp's anima, or speculate about his being a

multiple personality, an androgynous shaman, or a channel; Fiona, like the devas of Findhorn, is an otherworld
source of wisdom and information.

Months later, Elinore Detiger would write me a lengthy
letter that incorporated her thoughts and portions of Fiona
MacLeod's writing that she had gleaned from seven of her
books. Elinore wrote the following about Celtic revival:

> I believe that Celtic mythology is a living wellspring
> of thought forms and symbols which are at the root of
> what can be called Female Spirituality. The many-faceted
> Woman has generously been worshipped in Gaelic times.
> It is time to put Woman back on her pedestal, and there
> is no more beautiful way than the Celtic Way . . . the
> Celtic Triple Goddess. Brigit-Bride-Brighid. The broken
> old woman who is tired, has lost her beauty, and can no
> longer sing. The Sorrow, and yet the renewal and re-
> demption. In all her phases, she is Woman in glory and
> wisdom.
>
> The Celtic Legends carry a sweetness and a beauty
> which sings to all that is of music, of poetry, and of the
> heart . . . it touches the deepest and most mysterious as-
> pects of the human soul, our softest and most vulnerable
> parts.
>
> The emergence of Feminine Spirituality tells us of the
> Mother, the Mother of Song and Beauty. It tells us of the
> Lady of the Sea. . . . It tells us of the Woman, that is in
> the Heart of all Women.
>
> *Fiona MacLeod:* "I have thought often of old Mary
> Macarthur, and of her dream of holy St. Bride, and of
> that older Brigid of the West, Mother of Songs and
> Music—She who breathes in the reed, on the wind, in

the hearts of women and in the minds of poets. For I too, have my dream, my memory of one whom as a child I called Star-Eyes, and later called Banmorair-na-Mara, the Lady of the Sea, and whom at last I knew to be no other than the Woman that is in the heart of women."

Fiona MacLeod's vision: "I believe that we are close upon a great and deep spiritual change. I believe a new redemption is even now conceived of the Divine Spirit in the human heart, that is itself as a woman, broken in dreams and yet sustained in faith, patient, long-suffering, looking towards home. I believe that though the Reign of Peace may be yet a long way off, it is drawing near; and that Who shall save us anew shall come divinely as a Woman—but whether through mortal birth, or as an immortal breathing upon our souls, none can yet know. Sometimes I dream of the old prophecy that Christ shall come again upon Iona; and of that later prophecy which foretells, now as the Bride of Christ, now as the Daughter of God, now as the Divine Spirit embodied through mortal birth—the coming of a new Presence and Power, and dream that this may be upon Iona, so that the little Gaelic island may become as the little Syrian Bethlehem. But more wise is it to dream, not of hallowed ground, but of the hallowed gardens of the soul, wherein She shall appear white and radiant. Or that, upon the hills, where we wander, the Shepherdess shall call us home."

There are two images of the Goddess in Fiona MacLeod's writing that touch me: "the Woman that is in the heart of women" and "the Shepherdess who shall call us home." They both seem familiar to me. I have felt their presence, and I also recognize that they are archetypal images of the feminine and feminine divinity that is reemerging into consciousness, mostly through women. This Goddess is waiting for us to remember her. She is the divinity at Chartres who was there thousands of years before the cathedral was built. She is at the Clava Cairns and Glastonbury Tor. She is the Goddess who Morgaine realized would live on in Mary chapels in *The Mists of Avalon,* whose energy I felt at Pluscarden Abbey. She is the divinity of the heart in Celtic legends and the feminine aspect of God that I kept encountering on this pilgrimage.

Every time I sensed the sacredness of a place in my body, as I did for the first time in my life in Chartres Cathedral, it was literally a heartfelt experience. What came alive in me I could call "the Woman in the heart of women." I now understood the power behind the lines from Ntozake Shange's play *for colored girls who have considered suicide when the rainbow is enuf*: "I found god in myself, and I loved Her, I loved her fiercely."

We left Iona on a lovely morning, thankful for the serenity that pervades the place, that nourished us with its timelessness, for the invitation just to be, to neither have to go anywhere nor do anything. Iona was an island in time and a pause before the pilgrimage ended. In the midst of an unresolved and traumatic midlife transition, this part of the pilgrimage was deeply comforting.

We need time out of our everyday, outer-directed lives, and not just at major life transitions, when it is most advisable, but regularly. I think metaphorically of how necessary it is that we have "diastolic" time. For it is during diastole that the heart relaxes and fills. During systole, the heart contracts and sends a powerful stream of lifeblood out. For the heart to work and provide sustenance to the whole body, it must relax and fill. And so must we.

The Grail as a Discriminator of Truth

We took some sea-tumbled stones with us from Iona. Those made of Iona marble are baby-skin smooth to the touch, as soft and lovely as the spirit of the island; they feel feminine. The only other mementos of Iona came from a gift shop in the abbey and one small store near the ferry. Freya had bought a crystal chalice, which she carefully hand-carried in its box to the ferry, placing it where she thought it would be safe, but when someone moved our luggage, it broke. Its loss distressed her, and she wondered if there could be some meaning in it. She would later consign it to the sea on our much longer trip from Mull to Oban, when we were off the Northumberland coast near Bamburgh Castle, a place that was symbolically significant to her. Freya had also bought Iona mugs for each of us. They're the colors of Iona marble, white with soft-green markings, and almost too graceful to be called mugs. Later, her mug cracked and fragmented. Knowing of the symbolic connection between a chalice or a cup and the womb and already wondering about the broken chalice, Freya again contemplated what the message might be.

She saw these two episodes as metaphorically related to her hysterectomy. She thought that she could see a meaningful coincidence between the development of cancer in her uterus and what she was doing with her life; and she accepted that there were major changes to be made. For her as for me, the pilgrimage was a time for inner work in preparation for whatever was coming next in our lives, some of which we could anticipate. If she had had two dreams of broken vessels there would be no question that there was symbolic meaning to be found in them. She had a similar feeling about the broken chalice and mug.

Even before the pilgrimage, she had concluded that she needed to be more in touch with her feminine energies. She's a very feminine-looking person (many people comment that she looks like Guinevere) and a mother, but she claimed that she had lived too much in her head and intellect and had spent most of her time with men—working with men as colleagues, having men among her best friends, being married until recently, and having two sons and no daughters. This pilgrimage made her aware—as it did us all—of the mutually nurturing quality that is a significant part of women's friendships.

Living in her head and being the positive person she is, Freya reflected on how her mind, analytic intellect, and ability to see positive lessons in everything could override what her feelings and her body might be saying. Had she been truer to her feelings and acted from them, would she have stayed in situations that were negative, and did this contribute to the cancer? she wondered. Thoughts such as these cannot be proven. This way of thinking can be empowering and can lead to making important changes that serve us well; conversely, it can lead to destructive self-blame or blame-the-victim thinking.

There was no question in my mind about Freya's active intention to do whatever she needed to do to live fully and well. She *knew* that denying what she felt contributed to her illness, and that she needed to know what she felt and act accordingly. Both she and I had done the same thing with our feelings; we had disregarded them. I came to see that what I had always thought of as an altruistic and supportive instinct in me was not noble at all; that, rather, in denying my feelings and perceptions, I was being a co-dependent, lying to myself. Surprisingly, there is a mythological connection between an intact Grail and lying. In Celtic mythology one of the attributes of the Grail was as a discriminator of truth. In *The Grail Legend,* Emma Jung and Marie-Louise von Franz write:

> This was a crystal vessel or cup that had the peculiarity that when someone spoke three lying words it divided itself into three parts . . . and when anyone uttered three true words the pieces united again.:
>
> Through disintegration the vessel indicated that a lie was being told, and through unification it bore witness to the truth . . . he who lies deceives himself and disintegrates in the process, whereas he who tells the truth "heals" his soul and makes it whole.

I think of the lies that happen at the emotional or body level as a denial or repression of the truth of feelings, which we do unconsciously in the interest of maintaining harmony with significant people in our lives; or because the truth of what we feel isn't acceptable to us or others. Too often we do not even realize that we are being untrue to our authentic selves; we don't know that we are lying.

For example, in the period after I separated from my husband, I lied when I would say I was fine. It appeared to be true, even to me. But my body had become tense and fearful, and since my body seemed to be aware of feelings that the rest of me did not know, I began having body-work done to try to become aware.

One afternoon as I lay on the table for my session, I had an insight into the connection between feelings and body, and how disease could follow. I became aware that I was holding my left arm in such a way that it shielded my heart, with my left hand in a fist, the position of a shield-carrier. I had been through another difficult week and, as usual, stayed on top of things. However, as I lay there, I became aware not only of how I was holding my arm, but that if I opened and spread my arm like a wing, grief would well up. I also knew in that moment that I needed help to do it. I had too much resistance to opening up; some part of me was invested in keeping the feelings down, by keeping my shoulder and arm in the shield-holder position. I asked my body therapist if she would please move my arm up and off my chest. She did and the tears came.

As I struggled to open up and let the grief out, the physician-observer in me thought of the fairly common disease referred to either as a frozen shoulder or shoulder-hand syndrome. It's an excruciatingly painful condition experienced by some women in midlife. It often lasts as long as a year and then disappears as inexplicably as it came. Without physical therapy, muscle atrophy from disuse may complicate the condition. I think I could have been a candidate for this. The emotional pain I was not allowing myself to feel would then have expressed itself through my body as physical pain.

The lie I told myself was that I wasn't being traumatized, because I understood why the people I loved were behaving toward me as they were. And had I continued to be out of emotional touch, I think it might very well have been translated into physical disease. I think that this is the lie that causes the vessel to break, the disintegration to happen, and that it is a common condition.

Healing and reintegration of the psyche have to do with telling the truth. But it is a truth that often takes some doing to discover. It requires that we get in touch with what we really feel and face that we are in pain over something significant in our lives. The Perceval in us must ask, "What ails thee?" When we know, we will need to make changes in order to be true, which is to be healed.

The body can be a discriminator of truth; why it is for some people and not for others is an individual matter. When we repress feelings, memories, and perceptions, we lose our integrity as intact whole people and become divided, like the Grail, into separate parts. When we do this at the mental level, we split or dissociate; the psyche

breaks into parts, with information that we do not or cannot heed kept out of our conscious awareness. At the
physical level, symptoms, functional change, and physical
disease can result. Distress that we disown hurts us. When
it becomes impossible to live in a split-off way, the vessel
that is the mind, the heart, the soul, or the body can
"break."

FOURTEEN

Holy Island: Mother Earth

T he final destination of the
pilgrimage was Lindisfarne, or Holy Island. Lindisfarne is
clear across northern Scotland, practically due east from
Iona, off the eastern coast of northern England. (On our
way, we made one short stop to visit Rosslyn Chapel on
the outskirts of Edinburgh. I thought we did so only because it was a place of historical interest en route and was
not of sufficient significance to even mention as part of the

pilgrimage. Then I found in my reading of *The Holy Grail* by Norma Lorre Goodrich that the Holy Grail is supposedly contained in its Apprentice Pillar, and that initiate Knights Templar are still invested there into an ancient, holy Order of the Grail.) This reminded me how the mysterious Grail—as an experience of the Goddess—is hidden in places and people; a presence that is known and valued by the initiates, and missed and overlooked by anyone else.

Like Mont-Saint-Michel, the most famous of the holy islands in Europe, Lindisfarne can be reached only when the tide is out. On this last day of the pilgrimage, we left it up to synchronicity whether we would reach the island or not, since we didn't have access to a tide table. With the grace that had been with us this whole trip, we did in fact arrive just as the tide was coming in, while the road from the mainland was still passable.

We stopped at an inn for dinner. It had no rooms for guests but we found that lodging was available at Manor House, right next to the Lindisfarne Abbey ruins. We were in marvelous spirits, having driven across the beach road to Lindisfarne with the incoming tide practically lapping at our hubcaps. A group came into the inn, heard our laughter, and one of them said, "That's Jean Bolen's laugh!" They came into the dining room to see, and sure enough, my old friend Barbara Cook was right. Barbara had started the Friends of Jung of Greater Kansas City and mothered a fledgling group into an important resource for people on the individuation path. Seeing her reminded me once again of the network of light and how small the world is. And in that she is from the Jungian world, she was a bridging symbol for me, connecting the experience of pilgrimage with the goal of individuation.

When we are on an individuation path, there are several Jungian terms that express what the point of the journey is: circumambulating the Self; seeking wholeness by integrating the shadow; developing less conscious or undeveloped psychological functions (thinking, feeling, intuition, sensation), attitudes (extroverted, introverted), or qualities, masculine and feminine (anima and animus); becoming who we authentically are so that inner world and outer expression are in harmony. Pilgrimage, in Jungian terms, is an expression of and an effort to circumambulate the Self, to "quicken the divinity" by bringing the Self within us to life. Whether we call that part of us that seeks pilgrimage the soul or that part that seeks individuation the psyche, the meaning is the same and the goal is healing, wholeness, and transformation. The unexpected encounter with Barbara on Lindisfarne underscored this sameness.

Lindisfarne

Lindisfarne was founded in A.D. 635 when Saint Aiden came from Iona, shortly after war-torn Northumbria was reunited. Choosing the island as the site for his church and monastery, he established a center of Celtic Christianity that lasted for almost 250 years. Missionaries traveled from Lindisfarne throughout Britain and even journeyed to the Netherlands. The Lindisfarne Gospels, an illuminated manuscript as beautiful as the more famous Book of Kells, survives in the British Museum as one of the finest examples of Celtic art.

This center of spiritual light was invaded and plundered by the Vikings for the first time in A.D. 793. The light went out altogether in A.D. 875, when the remaining monks fled. For more than two centuries the island was uninhabited. Then in 1082, the Benedictines settled there once again and renamed it Holy Island.

Lindisfarne or Holy Island was another site built on ley lines. It was the last sacred place of our pilgrimage.

We stayed overnight, aware that we were cut off by the tide from the mainland. In the morning, the four of us spent time in the ruins of the priory, where I read "East Corker," the second of T. S. Eliot's *Four Quartets,* which explores the relationship of time to change and constancy. His images refer to buried life under what is now an open field, the dance that is life and the need for the soul to wait.

I said to my soul, be still, and wait without hope
For hope would be hope for the wrong thing; wait without
   love
For love would be love of the wrong thing; there is yet faith
But the faith and the love and the hope are all in the waiting.

Poetically it was appropriate for where we were—on Holy Island, cut off from the mainland, physically unable to move from where we were until the tides changed. Until then, we would have to wait. I was reminded by the geography that the pilgrimage itself had been a holy island of time in the midst of a major period of transition. In this period of my life, I was learning that I did not have control over what might happen next. In fact, I quite possibly could not even imagine it—which had certainly been the case when it came to this unexpected gift of pilgrimage.

Goddess and Gnosis

At the end of the pilgrimage, I looked back upon sacred places and sacred people and knew that this experience had been a great gift, the full meaning of which I might only receive over time. The Tiger Trust and the guiding hand of Elinore Detiger had made the pilgrimage possible; synchronicity and Mother Nature had blessed it. When I expressed my gratitude to Elinore, it led to a discussion that I have thought a lot about since. She said that I was not to think that this pilgrimage was something she had given to me personally, and that I was not indebted to her either, even though she had guided and accompanied me on this pilgrimage and would later bring me to pilgrimage sites in Greece, India, and Ireland. She did what she did, not for me as an individual nor to be acknowledged but because this was what she was to do. She was carrying out what she understood to be her assignment.

I think that there are some "assignments" that come to us and that we are free to accept or reject. Whether to accept each assignment is a soul-level choice. For example, one of my assignments was to speak up on behalf of women who had been sexually exploited in therapy by a prominent psychiatrist. That the psychiatrist had sexual relations with many of his women patients was well known and ignored by his and my colleagues, much as incest is ignored in dysfunctional families. While his behavior had been going on for years, I had not known of it until in a short span of time I became the recipient of a series of revelations: A woman in a seminar I was leading at the medical center spoke about the harm done to her by this man when he became sexual with her in her analysis after she had regressed and become a little girl who trusted him as a father; an analysand of mine told me about a woman whom he had just seen professionally who had become sexually involved with this same psychiatrist and what the consequences were to her; a colleague in my office building shared her distress about a patient she was seeing who had had sex with the psychiatrist in her therapy hours and had been obsessed and unable to go on with her life ever since. When I spoke about what I was hearing to another colleague, he told me that he had known better than to refer an attractive woman to the psychiatrist, that this was common knowledge. This knowledge was now unavoidably mine; that one after another person had brought their stories of this man to me felt like a series of synchronicities. I had a clear choice: to do something or do nothing.

The choice of what to do comes out of the complexities of our inner responses to outer events. Inside we are like a committee or a circle of personalities, archetypes, aspects, often with conflicting agendas and voices; who we listen to determines the path we take. I responded to "Silence is consent" and "All it takes for evil to prevail is for good women to do nothing," and I took on the assignment. I think that we do know what the soul calls upon us to do, and we can accept or reject it. Soul choices take us into the fire or into the void; they test our mettle and show us what kind of women we are, to paraphrase what Psyche was told as she undertook the four tasks in the myth of Eros and Psyche.

An assignment may be to act upon information that comes from outside us, as in my example. Or it may be to act upon an inner impression or intuition of what we are to do; many of Mrs. Detiger's assignments, of which I was one, were like this. Or they may be unavoidable, big, soul-testing events; the only choice we have then is how we will respond. Large or small, soul assignments are soul-shaping; they are how we learn; they may be what we came to do.

Extending the invitation to me to go on this pilgrimage was Elinore Detiger's assignment. Synchronicities made me aware that this was to be a significant journey. At the end of the pilgrimage, I realized that the times when I had opened my heart and felt the Goddess in embodied mystical experiences, which had led to my midlife crisis, had also made it possible for me to be a recipient of the energy that the Earth gives pilgrims at sacred sites. Without these experiences I would have been a tourist or researcher, not a pilgrim.

I have a sense that the Goddess—"the Woman that is in the heart of women"—is revealing herself to humankind again. She is appearing in our dreams as a numinous figure, sometimes as a larger-than-life dark woman, sometimes as a goddess, sometimes as a guide. "The Woman that is in the heart of women" is an inner figure. She is feminine wisdom, knowledge that comes through the heart, a way of knowing that became discounted and devalued with patriarchy, which substituted obedience to outer authority for this inner knowing. In Greek mythology, she was Metis, the Goddess of Wisdom, whom Zeus tricked into becoming small and swallowed when she was pregnant with Athena. She was Sophia, whom the church fathers banished along with the Gnostic heresies, and she was the Shekinah, the forgotten feminine face of God in Judaism.

A gnostic way of knowing is feminine wisdom. Elaine Pagels in *The Gnostic Gospels* has this to say about the Gnostics:

> These Christians are now called gnostics, from the Greek word gnosis, usually translated as "knowledge." But gnosis is not primarily rational knowledge. The Greek language distinguishes between scientific or reflective knowledge ("He knows mathematics") and knowing through observation or experience ("He knows me"),

which is gnosis. As gnostics use the term, we could translate it as "insight," for gnosis involves an intuitive process of knowing oneself. And to know oneself, they claimed, is to know human nature and human destiny . . . to know oneself, at the deepest level, is simultaneously to know God; this is the secret of gnosis.

The Gnostic gospels, known also as the Nag Hammadi scrolls, were discovered and translated in the mid-twentieth century, which meant that they came to light only when there was science and scholarship available to preserve and translate them. Furthermore, that the women's movement was under way when they became available for study meant that there were women scholars to work on them and a change in consciousness that allowed at least partial receptivity to the emergence of Sophia or feminine wisdom from repression by the early church fathers.

The Earth Is Our Mother

The photo of the Earth taken from outer space may be the most significant image in the evolution of human consciousness in the twentieth century; it was a gift from Apollo—NASA's Apollo space missions. The Apollo astronauts saw the Earth from outer space for the first time. And through them, we could see the Earth as a holy island against a sea of blackness, a sunlit ocean-blue globe with swirls of clouds and glimpses of continents. This image of the Earth touched the heart and brought humanity into a planetary age, with the psychological awareness that we share the fate of the earth, which has finite resources.

Russell Schweickart and Edgar Mitchell were two of the Apollo astronauts, and they have spoken publicly of the spiritual transformations that took place in them when they looked at the earth from outer space. Schweickart had five unscheduled minutes in outer space when a camera he was carrying failed; while he waited for it to be fixed or replaced, he held onto a rung of the ladder and turned to face the Earth. At the time, he was testing a life-support system, and so he was also the first astronaut ever to be outside the spacecraft without an umbilical cord.

Schweickart has the soul of a poet, for he realized,

> I was literally in the position, at that moment, of representing everybody else on the surface of the earth. My obligation was to absorb that experience of looking at the Earth from outer space. I didn't try to do a lot of processing of it. I just tried to completely open up . . . since then I've spent a lot of time integrating that five minutes into the rest of my life and trying to really work through what it means for all of us.

Until we gain some distance from Mother, we cannot see her at all. For the infant, mother is food, warmth, comfort; she is the environment. The child and the adolescent see the personal mother more distinctly than the infant, but not by much, in that she is indistinguishable from the maternal environment she provides. The same applies to adults who continue to see and react to their mothers from child places in their psyches. At what point do we see our mother's face and realize that she is a unique person who gave us birth, loves us, is beautiful in our eyes and vulnerable, and know that time and work have taken a toll on her and that someday she may need us to look after her?

Not until we could venture into outer space and look back upon the Earth could humankind have a similar experience of Mother Earth. The beautiful blue and white planet that is earth, a sphere glowing with light, silhouetted against the blackness of space, is a gorgeous sight. She is beautiful and vulnerable, and the only Mother Earth we have.

In photographs, Earth also has the shape of a mandala, a circle within a square, the symbol of what Jung called the Self, an image of wholeness and the archetype of meaning. The Self is whatever we experience that is greater than our small selves through which we know that there is something meaningful to our existence. The round or the circle is a feminine symbol that represented the Great Mother before humanity could know that the Earth is round. The Earth is the Great Mother Goddess: she births us and breathes us and feeds us and holds us to her body with gravity, and we return to her in death.

The Goddess makes the body and life sacred, and connects us to the divinity that permeates all matter; her symbolic organ is the womb. We can know her gnostically through the divine daughter or Grail Maiden, the carrier of awareness of feminine divinity, "the Woman in the heart of women." Her organ of knowledge is the heart. Both heart and womb are vessels through which life is animated. They are both chalices for blood that fill and empty. One sustains life, the other brings new life forth.

FIFTEEN

Down to Earth: Return

T he time comes for the pilgrim to return from the pilgrimage, for the astronaut to reenter the earth's atmosphere and splash down, for mythological Apollo to come back from the Hyperboreans to Delphi, and for Perceval's quest to end.

When I returned home to California and went to the market for groceries something curious happened. I looked at the well-stocked meat section where I usually picked up steaks, and my body said, "No, thank you." Before the pilgrimage, it had been my habit to eat a small New York steak for breakfast every morning. Champagne was my other dietary idiosyncrasy. Once I discovered that a pressure-maintaining stopper kept it bubbly, a bottle of champagne always had a place in my refrigerator. A glass or two in the evening was a small pleasure. From the first evening back, however, champagne was no longer appealing, either.

My mind didn't have anything to do with these dietary decisions. No willpower was involved. I followed what my body wanted, and the thinking, observing part of me just watched. I was reminded of something I was told in medical school, of an experiment with older infants who had been breast-fed exclusively and then could choose what solid food they would eat. It might have been beets for a week or whatever. But the babies instinctively seemed to choose what they needed nutritionally. Might it be that we can instinctively know what our bodies need?

I wondered at my own instinctive response at the meat counter and refrigerator. Did it have to do with something my body knew it needed in order to stay healthy? Or, since I'm intellectually aware that many people who have a spiritual practice do not eat meat or drink alcohol, was my body making an instinctive spiritual decision? I did not know why, but that I could listen and heed what it was my body wanted was in itself a new experience in awareness.

First the "tuning fork" body response to sacred places, and now this. On returning, I not only had a deep con-

nection to Earth as Mother, but I found that I had also ac-
quired a different relationship to my own "earth," my
body. By paying attention to how my body responded to
places and trusting her to know what my mind could not,
I had opened a way to know myself and know what mattered. Just as "matter" and "mother" come from the same
root word, so do the earth and the body belong to the
mother realm.

Instinctual Choices

With my mystical bent and my affinity for the archetypal
world, the down-to-earthness of focusing on what I eat
seems pretty mundane—and then, as I think about it,
pretty wonderful. I was learning how to tell what is truly
nourishing and good for me from what isn't. Listening to
the earth, heeding my body's knowledge, I was uncovering
an Earth Mother hidden in my unconscious.

The same gentle "no, thank you" response to red meat
and alcohol persisted for three years, and then one day I
opened the stoppered bottle of champagne that had sat in
a corner of my refrigerator this whole time, found it still
had some bubbles, and poured myself some; on another
occasion, a meat dish was appealing and with the same
lack of fanfare I said, "Thank you, I'll have some."

What I choose or refuse to put in my mouth and take
into my body is tangible and visible. On the pilgrimage, I
went to sacred sites and absorbed the invisible nourishment that I sensed was there. It was soul food, Mother's

milk to nourish the divinity within the pilgrim. The practice at these sites of having my body do the perceiving carried over into ordinary life and applied to choosing ordinary food.

Purification: Removing Obstacles to Clarity

It is not easy to recognize and choose good nourishment of any kind if the spontaneous and receptive instinctual part of us is numb and neglected. I look back to Glastonbury, to the ritual that began with purification in the Chalice Well garden. And I think of it now as both a powerful ritual in itself and a naming of what I was unknowingly already engaged in. "Purification" has to do with removing the obstacles to clarity, of getting back to one's true self.

For some it requires going to a detoxification center in order to become clean and free of what is addictive and numbing. For many clarity comes through a commitment to a psychotherapeutic process. For me, the most important means was the solitude and sanctuary that I had unexpectedly found in moving to a place of my own. Where the space I fell asleep in and awoke in was uncluttered, and everything was aesthetically and symbolically pleasing; where my energy or soul field did not merge with or react to anyone else's; where I could be in my own aura. I believe that this period of solitude was an essential preparation for the pilgrimage that allowed me to be open and in the moment, receptive and unarmored; this and the company of women who were not seeking anything from me and with whom I could be myself. No one of us had to be the mother or the child or the wisewoman, all were welcomed presences; we were all pilgrims who appreciated the company of the others, and respected the necessity for solitude as well.

I know that it is extremely important to be alone for a time, to have a time and place apart; to be as if on Iona, away from the mainland, away from the scheduled interactive life, away from other people's energies, needs, and projections. I found that solitude gives me myself for company, and that when I am alone, especially in the early morning, that it is as if I am a deep quiet pool that allows whatever needs to come into my awareness to surface.

Only by being inwardly attentive can we learn to tell what we should take in, who feels safe to be with, where we want to be, what is true for us. Whatever it is we must do to reach the knower of truth in ourselves is our particular "purification." Purification has to do with intention and preparation, the removal of barriers and contaminants, until we can respond authentically to what we encounter.

To respond authentically to what we enounter: this is how we all reacted as children, before we were punished or shamed for doing so. To respond authentically to what we encounter—how hard it is for adults to do something that sounds so simple. To do so, we *only* have to be inwardly attentive, we *only* have to know what we feel, we *only* have to be able to respond with an innocent, spontaneous, instinctive receptivity that is a finely attuned discriminating consciousness, a body and soul reaction to the world around us.

We can only afford to be this conscious if we can act upon what we perceive. To respond authentically to what we enounter has to do with choice, with having the power to act upon what we know. It is as simple as being able to take in or refuse the food we are offered and as complex as our responses to the complex elements that comprise our lives.

The Child Who Knows

The child who instinctively knows the truth about what she loves and who loves her, also responds to stories that are *true* in the deepest mythical sense. For us to do the same, we need to be both the child within us that is open to wonder and magic, who listens uncritically and enters the story *for real,* and a wiseperson who knows that the story is true metaphorically.

Madeleine L'Engle writes in the children's story *A Ring of Endless Light:*

> Grandfather reprimanded: "You have to give the darkness permission. It cannot take over otherwise."
>
> But I hadn't given it permission. It had come as suddenly and unexpectedly as death had come and taken the child in my arms.
>
> "Vicky, do not add to the darkness."
>
> I heard him and did not hear him.
>
> "Vicky, this is my charge to you. You are to be a lightbearer. You are to choose the light."

"I can't . . . ," I whispered.

"You already have. I know that from your poems. But it is a choice which you must renew now."

I remember being in the audience in a darkened theater watching *Peter Pan,* when Tinkerbell's light flickered and went out. Only if we all believed could she come to life again; only if we all said it out loud would the magic work. It felt as if everyone in the audience became a child who said, "I believe" as with one voice, which caused her light to glow brightly once more.

When the light in anyone flickers and an immense and hopeless darkness looms threateningly close, it is her soul, not her physical body, that is like Tinkerbell. It is at these times that someone else's love and belief in us can really help, when a story can make a difference.

Remember Walt Disney's Dumbo, the little elephant with the enormous ears who couldn't fly until a crow who believed he could gave him a feather to hold in his trunk and told him it was magic? Thinking that the feather made it possible to fly, Dumbo flapped his ears and took off; this was what he needed to do, what he had the ability to do all along. What made him special made him different. Like Rudolph the Rednosed reindeer's glowing nose, Dumbo's big floppy ears made him different, and the discrepancy between himself and others made him ashamed.

Without the feather, Dumbo would never have taken off; he would never have known the joy of flying. He needed something to hold on to in order to believe that he could be the unique elephant he was. That feather may be a myth or a fairy tale, an image from a motion picture, or a theme from a novel that is grasped by the soul. Or, as countless people know from listening to each other tell the truth of their own lives, it can be a story told by the person who lived it that sustains another person on her own journey. In women's circles and men's groups, in recovery groups all over the world modeled on Alcoholics Anonymous, people are telling each other their stories.

In my analytic practice, I have learned how a story told by a rejected or abused child to herself can get her through childhood with her soul intact. Abused children usually decide that they must be bad to deserve the bad treatment they are getting. They accept verbal abuse as the truth about their badness or worthlessness. With abusive adults as role models, they are likely to grow up to become abusive adults themselves. There are exceptions: while abuse always leaves emotional scars, a child who can tell herself a story such as "these people are not my people; when I grow up I will find my real family someday" may make the story come true. She fantasizes parents who are loving and inwardly identifies with them rather than her own abusive parents. Like a prisoner of war whose spirit is not broken because he believes that if he just endures or escapes, he will be reunited with his own people, a child's personal version of this story prevents her from accepting an abusive family's reality as her own.

Survival of a child's soul or her innocence in the face of circumstances that would otherwise make her cynical or despairing, depends upon holding on to a personal myth and has to do with having an inviolate inner life. The inner world of imagination becomes a sanctuary of hope and promise, a place of retreat for feelings and thoughts, where seeds of individuality and creativity incubate.

Living for at least five thousand years in cultures where there is no Goddess, no reverence for childbearing and child rearing, where dominating the earth and women is theologically sanctioned and men demonstrate their manhood through war and other equivalent rites of passage, *any woman, no matter how personally privileged, is spiritually oppressed.* Under patriarchy, women become alienated from other women and from our own bodies. That which makes us different from men makes us feel inferior and ashamed, as does that which we do that men don't accept in women.

I believe that the fantasy novel *The Clan of the Cave Bear* by Jean Auel became a runaway best-seller for the same reasons as did *The Mists of Avalon.* Women readers found personally relevant this metaphorically true story, and we responded. *The Clan of the Cave Bear* takes place in a time of transition, this time a transition in human evolution. The protagonist Ayla is rejected and punished because she acts differently from how females are supposed to act; she is "other." Ayla's story is the story child survivors tell themselves. Orphaned as a child, she is with people who are not her people. In spite of abuse, she does not lose courage or her capacity to love. By the end of the novel, she sets out on her own to find people like herself. Significantly, what sets Ayla apart is what sets women apart from men in patriarchy. She is derided for her expressiveness and emotionality, for her laughter and tears, for her ability and desire to communicate feelings, for her curiosity. She observes and reasons instead of taking authority's word for how things are and how they are done, develops skills that are considered the exclusive realm of men, finds creative solutions, and fears that she will be punished or ostracized if people know what she is doing.

I read Clarissa Pinkola Estés's richly metaphoric descriptions of the Wild Woman in *Women Who Run with the Wolves* and recognized that she was the Goddess in another of her myriad manifestations and names. For example, Estés says of the Wild Woman: "She is the source of the feminine. She is all that is of instinct, of the worlds both seen and hidden—she is the basis." "She encourages humans to remain multilingual; fluent in the languages of dreams, passions, and poetry." "She is ideas, feelings, urges, and memory. She has been lost and half forgotten for a long, long time."

The Wild Woman that Estés writes of is that part of a woman that knows the truth, that has access to her instinctual feminine nature and the archetypal realm, and can tap into the wisdom of the body and soul. This Wild Woman—from the perspective of Avalon—is also that part of a woman that recognizes the Goddess, and in embodied sacred moments, becomes the Goddess.

A story that truly sustains us on a soul-chosen path rings deeply true and is a source of inspiration, hope, and meaning. When I read *Passages About Earth* by William

Irwin Thompson, there were words from his synopsis of a book by Doris Lessing that leaped off the page because they fit the images and intuitions that I had on this pilgrimage. I have exercised poetic license in excerpting and italicizing what struck me to read as follows:

> Once upon a time the gods gathered and decided to send yet another mission to Planet Earth. A briefing was held to prepare for the descent. Those that would go chose to become human and would have to lose all memory of their divinity. *Their task would be to discover one another on earth, recover their memories through intuition, and piece together the members of the descent.*
>
> *In the darkness that covered the earth, these individuals and sacred places were points of scattered light in a web which bound the dark:* a scattering of people, a light webby tension of them everywhere over the globe.

Telling Our Own Story

The pilgrimage I describe in this book took place in May 1986. I wrote the first draft of this book between December 1986 and April 1987, and then put it away until the beginning of 1990, when I thought I was ready to work on it again. Life intervened. My son had major surgery in the spring, and he needed me then and through his recuperation and graduation from high school. As both a mother and a medical doctor, my heart and head and energies were primarily engaged in accompanying him through this part of his journey. Summer came, and with it came

time to write again, except that in June I became en-
thralled by Richard Wagner's opera cycle, *The Ring of the
Nibelung,* which I saw as a commentary on patriarchy and
dysfunctional relationships. It took over my creative
process as if it were an unplanned pregnancy, and I instead
wrote *Ring of Power: The Abandoned Child, The Authori-
tarian Father, and the Disempowered Feminine,* which was
published in 1992.

In January 1993, I opened the carton in which I was
storing the first draft of *Crossing to Avalon* and my notes
and thoughts about revising it from the abortive attempt
in 1990, read through what I had written, and knew that it
needed only some minor additions and deletions. Many
books have been published about the Earth as Gaia, femi-
nist theology, goddess archaeology, women's spirituality,
planetary consciousness, deep ecology, paradigm shifts,
and other areas of thought that support the thesis of an
emerging "goddess consciousness." My story tells how it
happened for me.

It wasn't that this manuscript needed six years of work
before it was ready. I needed the time to move through
"the forest" phase of my life, see my two children become
solid young adults, and overcome my reluctance to accept
the "assignment" of telling my own story, which goes
against the grain of my training in psychiatry and against
my family tradition of privacy.

I have been in excellent health during the eight years
since the pilgrimage; the potential for serious illness seen

by the sensitive in the Netherlands did not materialize. I may very well have been at a crossroads and taken a path that took me away from that possibility. I made changes in how I lived, entered an easy menopause, and began to keep company with a joyful inner child. Freya, whose 50/50 cancer prognosis positioned her at the crossroads between life and death, took the life road and passed the five-year survival marker more than four years ago.

We both came into the realm of the archetype of Hecate, the crone and wisewoman, Greek Goddess of the Crossroads, who also symbolizes the postmenopausal period. I had my last menstrual period at Glastonbury; Freya's hysterectomy brought about a premature surgical menopause.

Hecate was a powerful pre-Olympian divinity who, positioned at the fork in the road, could see where the traveler was coming from and where each of the two roads she could choose from would take her. Hecate could look down all three roads, *tri-via* in Latin; like all prepatriarchal goddesses, she became *trivialized*. As an archetype, she exists in the liminal place between day and night consciousness, in the half-light of imagination, intuition, and vision. As a goddess, she was associated with caves, which are symbolic of the womb and tomb of the Great Mother, the interface between the underworld and the upper world. In a culture that fears and negates old women, the goddess Hecate became caricaturized as an ugly hag stirring her cauldron, a coming together of Greek and Celtic mythology, of Hecate and Cerridwen the Celtic Great

Mother whose cauldron of plenty, of regeneration and rebirth, inspiration and wisdom, was the pre-Christian Grail.

Periods of darkness, times in the forest and the underworld, are times when we are in the cauldron, more aware than during ordinary times of the necessity and possibility of regeneration and healing, in the place of surrender and choice.

To be vulnerable and fallible, to have a shadow and a soul, to make our way through life determining who we become by the choices we make, is what we do here. Over and over again, it seems to me, life comes along and says, "Choose!" The small and large moments of truth that shape what goes into or is left out of a book, find parallels in the small and large moments of truth that go into the choices we make in life about what to add or delete. These are the decisions that shape our lives, which ultimately are soul journeys.

If the Goddess is to return to the world as the Grail that will heal the patriarchy, if the Goddess is to come into human consciousness as an awareness of the sacred feminine in her myriad expressions, if the Goddess is to emerge in time, she will do so because women and men tell what they know. The Goddess comes to us in very private and experiential ways. *To bring about a paradigm shift in the culture that will change assumptions and attitudes, a critical number of us have to tell the stories of our personal revelations and transformations.*

I have kept *Crossing to Avalon* close to my heart, for it is a sacred part of my personal story that has until now been a very private part of my life. Wherever it goes, I hope that it will be treated gently, but more than that, I hope that my story will remind you of or waken you to your own soul journey and the revelatory moments and deep truths that are your own particular glimpse of the Grail or experience of the Goddess.

In Barry Lopez's allegorical fable *Crow and Weasel,* two friends are returning home after a long journey when they meet Badger. They tell her where they have been and what has happened to them. She knows that it is not just the journey but the story that is important and tells them why:

> The stories people tell have a way of taking care of them. If stories come to you, care for them. And learn to give them away where they are needed. Sometimes a person needs a story more than food to stay alive.

Love to you on *your* journey.

Acknowledgments

To Elinore Detiger, whose guiding hand, wise heart, and generosity were the means through which I have gotten a larger vision of the world and my place in it.

To Marion Zimmer Bradley for *The Mists of Avalon,* which inspired me to think of the Grail legend from a Goddess perspective.

To Freya Reeves, Soozi Holbeche, and Elinore Detiger, my sister pilgrims, whose lives, honesty, humor, wisdom, and adventuresome spirits made our journey together the shared, spontaneous, and sacred experience it was.

To my friends who saw me through chapters in my life and/or read through the chapters in my book and helped them turn out as they have: Patricia Ellerd, Sherry Anderson, Pauline Tesler, Toni Triest, Pat Hopkins, China Galland, Helen Stolfus, Isabel Allende, Clarissa Pinkola Estés, Cornelia Schulz, Kay Hensley, Valerie Andrews, Alice Walker, Arisika Razak, Elaine Viseltear, Jan Lovett-Keen.

To my mother, Megumi Y. Shinoda, M.D., for her continued support in my life, even when it was especially difficult and for a time, beyond understanding; for reading two earlier versions, contributing her perspective, and leaving me psychologically free to write whatever I thought important.

To my daughter Melody and my son Andre, for their unconditional love and loyalty, through whom I became a mother with all that it has brought.

To the people at HarperSanFrancisco who transform my writing into books and get them out into the world. My editor, Caroline Pincus, whose meticulous care with the text, willingness to dialogue over differences, availability, and encouragement made her a worthy and appreciated midwife for this book. A fine copyediting hand and eye for detail was added by Lorraine Anderson. My publishers: Clayton E. Carlson, the publisher of all of my books before this one, beginning with *The Tao of Psychology*, who let me temporarily abandon working on *Gods in Everyman* in order to write *Crossing to Avalon*, saying—as I recall—that "the best books are written when an author is in the grip of a creative process." Clayton read the first draft, believed in it, and let it come to fruition in its own, or my, time. Now that he has larger responsibilities at HarperCollins, Tom Grady, my former editor for *Goddesses in Everywoman*, *Gods in Everyman*, and *Ring of Power*, is my publisher and I feel his continued support. The title came up during a staff meeting and is the inspiration of Brenda Knight. Production editing went smoothly thanks to Terri Goff's coordination and communication. Once created and named, the baby that is a new book is given into the care of promotion and marketing, who see it into the world; for past as well as present effort, I thank Ani Chamichian and Robin Seaman and their staffs.

To Betty Karr, my executive assistant, for her help with my work, for transcribing the first draft of this book onto a disk, and for taking care of the logistics of much of my professional life, which enables me to have more time to do creative work and have time for myself.

To people whose gifts got incorporated into this book: my daughter Melody for Madeleine L'Engle's *A Ring of Endless Light*. Gerry Oliva's gift was Mary Oliver's "The Journey." Corey Fischer's production of *Sometimes a Person Needs a Story More Than Food* for the Travelling Jewish Theater brought Barry Lopez's *Crow and Weasel* into my awareness. Other individuals who contributed to the contents include Jo Norris, Clare Heriza, Don Mechling, Anthea Francine, and Trish Honea-Fleming.

To people who have written to me and not gotten a reply: a thank-you and an explanation. I don't seem to be able to write a book and answer correspondence at the same time (though I usually read all my mail). Occasionally I do respond because of something in the timing, the letter, and my psyche; under such circumstances, I hope that synchronicity is playing an unseen hand in this otherwise poor performance.

For more about synchronicity, my book, *The Tao of Psychology: Synchronicity and the Self,* provides an intellectual, spiritual, and psychological perspective on this subject, which had such a prominent part in the events to do with *Crossing to Avalon.*

ACKNOWLEDGMENTS

When pilgrims or trekkers pass each other on the path in the Himalayas, they bow to one another and say "Namaste," which means "The divinity in me acknowledges the divinity in thee," or "The God in me greets the God in thee." If you have taken the words in my book to heart and felt what I have described, let us have this greeting as we pass: "The Goddess in me beholds the Goddess in thee." *Namaste.*

JEAN SHINODA BOLEN

References

Epigraph

Walker, Alice. "Interview," *Common Boundary* (March-April, 1990): 19.

Chapter 1   Invitation: Pilgrimage

Bolen, Jean Shinoda. *Goddesses in Everywoman.* San Francisco: Harper & Row, 1984.

Campbell, Joseph. *The Hero with a Thousand Faces.* Bollingen Series 17. Princeton, NJ: Princeton University Press, 1949, pp. 51, 55.

Daumal, René. *Mount Analogue: A Novel of Symbolically Authentic Non-Euclidean Adventures in Mountain Climbing.* Translation and introduction by Roger Shattuck, with a postface by Vera Daumal. New York: Penguin Books, 1983 (originally published in French by Librairie Gallimard, Paris, 1952), pp. 66, 67, 112.

Eliot, T. S. "The Dry Salvages," lines 201–202. In *Four Quartets.* New York: Harcourt Brace Jovanovich, 1943, p. 44.

Stein, Murray. *In Midlife: A Jungian Perspective.* Dallas: Spring Publications, 1983.

Chapter 2   Meeting: The Dalai Lama

Guthrie, W.K.C. *The Greeks and Their Gods.* Boston: Beacon Press, 1950, pp. 78–79.

Hicks, Roger, and Ngakpa Chogyam. *Great Ocean: An Authorized Biography of the Buddhist Monk Tenzin Gyatso, His Holiness the*

Fourteenth Dalai Lama. Great Britain: Element Books, 1984, pp. 168, 169.

Chapter 3   Quickening: Chartres Cathedral

Adams, Henry. *Mont-Saint-Michel and Chartres.* Introduction by Lord Briggs. New York: Gallery Books, W. H. Smith, 1985 (originally published 1913), p. 68.

Charpentier, Louis. *The Mysteries of Chartres Cathedral.* Translated by Ronald Fraser. New York: Avon Books, 1975, pp. 20, 9, 20.

Kern, Hermann. *Labyrinthe.* Munich: Prestel-Verlage, 1983, p. 206. (Contains lists, text, and photographs of labyrinth sites in Europe.)

Male, Emile. *Chartres.* Translated by Sarah Wilson. New York: Harper & Row, 1983, p. 9.

Walker, Barbara G. *The Women's Encyclopedia of Myths and Secrets.* San Francisco: Harper & Row, 1983, p. 523.

Chapter 4   The Grail Legend: The Spiritual Journey

Bolen, Jean Shinoda. *The Tao of Psychology.* San Francisco: Harper & Row, 1979, pp. 99–101.

———. *Goddesses in Everywoman,* p. 145.

Bradley, Marion Zimmer. *The Mists of Avalon.* New York: Ballantine Books, 1982, p. 771.

de Troyes, Chrétien. *Perceval or The Story of the Grail.* Translated by Ruth Harwood Cline. Athens, GA: University of Georgia Press, 1985.

Jung, Emma, and Marie-Louise von Franz. *The Grail Legend* (2nd ed.). Translated by Andrea Dykes. Boston: Sigo Press, 1986 (originally published in 1960 as *Die Graalslegend in psychologischer Sicht,* Zurich and Stuttgart, in the series Studiem aus dem C. G. Jung-Institut, XII).

Matthews, John. *The Grail: Quest for the Eternal.* New York: Crossroad, 1981, p. 62.

References

Chapter 5 Women's Mysteries and the Grail

Bolen, Jean Shinoda. *Goddesses in Everywoman.*

Demetrakopoulos, Stephanie. *Listening to Our Bodies: The Rebirth of Feminine Wisdom.* Boston: Beacon Press, 1983, pp. 43, 43–44, 41.

Eliot, T. S. "The Dry Salvages," lines 93–95. In *Four Quartets,* p. 39.

Gimbutas, Marija. *The Language of the Goddess.* San Francisco: Harper & Row, 1989, p. 141.

Harding, M. Esther. *Woman's Mysteries: Ancient and Modern.* New York: G. P. Putnam's Sons for the C. G. Jung Foundation for Analytical Psychology, 1971.

Homer. *The Homeric Hymns* (2nd ed., Revised). "Hymn to Demeter (I)." Translated by Charles Boer. Irving, TX: Spring Publications, 1979, p. 129.

Kerenyi, C. *Eleusis: Archetypal Image of Mother and Daughter.* Translated by Ralph Manheim. New York: Schocken Books, 1977, pp. 9, 17.

Webster's Tenth New Collegiate Dictionary. Springfield, MA: Merriam-Webster, 1993, p. 770.

Chapter 6 Pilgrimage to Glastonbury

Ashe, Geoffrey. *Avalonian Quest.* London: Methuen London, 1982. Fontana, 1984, p. 140, illustration 8 (between pp. 144 and 145).

Bolen, Jean Shinoda. "Synchronicity and the Tao: Mysticism, Metaphor, Morphic Fields and the Quest for Meaning," *ReVision* 16:1 (Summer 1993): 8–14.

Bond, Frederick Bligh. *The Gate of Remembrance: The Story of the Psychological Experiment which Resulted in the Discovery of the Edgar Chapel at Glastonbury* (5th ed.). Wellingborough, Northamptonshire, England: Thorson's, 1978 (originally published 1918).

Michell, John. *New Light on the Ancient Mystery of Glastonbury.* England: Gothic Image, 1990.

Sheldrake, Rupert. *A New Science of Life: The Hypothesis of Formative Causation*. Los Angeles: Tarcher, 1981.

———. "Mind, Memory, and Archetype," *Psychological Perspectives* 18:1 (Spring 1987): 9–25.

———. "Society, Spirit, and Ritual," *Psychological Perspectives* 18:2 (Fall 1987): 320–331.

Chapter 7   Sister Pilgrims: Glastonbury Tales

Ashe, Geoffrey. *Avalonian Quest.*

Bond, Frederick Bligh. *The Gate of Remembrance.*

Bradley, Marion Zimmer. *The Mists of Avalon*, p. 133.

Fortune, Dion. *Glastonbury: Avalon of the Heart*. Wellingborough, Northamptonshire, England: Aquarian Press, 1989 (originally published as *Avalon of the Heart*, 1934), pp. 19–20.

Walker, Barbara G. *The Women's Encyclopedia of Myths and Secrets*, pp. 1045–46.

Chapter 8   Avalon: Otherworld and Motherworld

Ashe, Geoffrey. *Avalonian Quest.*

Bradley, Marion Zimmer. *The Mists of Avalon*, pp. 131, 132, x.

Campbell, Joseph. *Transformations of Myth Through Time*. New York: Harper & Row, 1990, p. 237.

Jung, Emma, and Marie-Louise von Franz. *The Grail Legend*, p. 66.

Chapter 9   In the Forest: Midlife Landscape

Bly, Robert. *Iron John*. Reading, MA: Addison-Wesley, 1990.

Blum, Ralph. *The Book of Runes*. A Handbook for the Use of an Ancient Oracle: The Viking Runes. New York: St. Martin's Press, 1982.

Estés, Clarissa Pinkola. *Women Who Run with the Wolves*. New York: Ballantine, 1993, pp. 387–455.

The I Ching. The Richard Wilhelm Translation rendered into English by Cary F. Baynes (Third Edition). Bollingen Series XIX, Princeton, NJ: Princeton University Press, 1967.

References

Neumann, Erich. *Amor and Psyche: The Psychic Development of the Feminine.* Bollingen Series 54. Translated by Ralph Manheim. New York: Pantheon, 1956.

Oliver, Mary. "The Journey." In *Dream Work.* New York: The Atlantic Monthly Press, 1986, pp. 38–39.

Chapter 10   The Wasteland: Depression and Despair

Andrews, Lynn V. *Jaguar Woman.* San Francisco: Harper & Row, 1985, pp. 43–49.

Bly, Robert. *Sleepers Holding Hands.* New York: Harper & Row, 1985 (originally published 1973), pp. 29–50.

The Family of Man. The greatest photographic exhibition of all time—503 pictures from 68 countries—created by Edward Steichen for the Museum of Modern Art. New York: Museum of Modern Art, 1955.

Chapter 11   Circumambulation: London

Frank, Anne. *The Diary of a Young Girl.* Translated by B.M. Mooyaaart. New York: Pocket Books, 1972 (originally published in 1947 as *Het Achterhuis,* Amsterdam: Contact), p. 237.

Lewis, C. S. *Till We Have Faces: A Myth Retold.* San Diego, CA: Harcourt Brace, 1957, pp. 270–272.

Chapter 12   The Greening of the Wasteland: Findhorn

Findhorn Community. *Faces of Findhorn: Images of a Planetary Family.* New York: Harper & Row, 1980, pp. 129, 169–75.

Fox, Matthew. "Viriditas: Greening Power" and "Sin—Drying Up." In *Illuminations of Hildegard of Bingen.* Text by Hildegard of Bingen with commentary by Matthew Fox. Santa Fe, NM: Bear & Co., 1985, pp. 30–37, 63–65.

Jung, Emma, and Marie-Louise von Franz. *The Grail Legend,* p. 165.

Koestler, Arthur. *The Robot and the Lotus.* New York: Harper & Row, 1960.

Chapter 13   Musings: Iona and Other Sacred Places

Bradley, Marion Zimmer. *The Mists of Avalon,* p. 875.

Jung, Emma, and Marie-Louise von Franz. *The Grail Legend,* p. 135.

Shange, Ntozake. *for colored girls who have considered suicide when the rainbow is enuf.* New York: Macmillan, 1976.

Chapter 14   Holy Island: Mother Earth

Eliot, T. S. "East Corker," lines 125–32. In *Four Quartets,* p. 28.

Goodrich, Norma Lorre. *The Holy Grail.* New York: Harper-Collins, 1992, p. 327.

Michell, John. "Lindisfarne." In *The Traveler's Key to Sacred England.* New York: Knopf, 1988, pp. 235–41.

Pagels, Elaine. *The Gnostic Gospels.* New York: Random House, 1979, p. xix.

Schweickart, Russell. "No Frames, No Boundaries." In *Earth's Answer:* Explorations of Planetary Culture at the Lindisfarne Conference. Editors: Michael Katz, Willima P. Marsh, Gail Gordon Thompson. New York: Lindisfarne Press, 1977. (The quote is from an informal talk, the content and context is in this essay.)

Chapter 15   Down to Earth: Return

Auel, Jean. *The Clan of the Cave Bear.* New York: Bantam, 1984.

Estés, Clarissa Pinkola. *Women Who Run with the Wolves.* New York: Ballantine, 1992, p. 13.

L'Engle, Madeleine. *A Ring of Endless Light.* New York: Dell, 1981, pp. 325–26.

Lopez, Barry. *Crow and Weasel.* San Francisco: North Point Press, 1990, p. 48.

Thompson, William Irwin. *Passages About Earth.* New York: Harper & Row, 1973, pp. 136–37. (This is Thompson's description of Doris Lessing's *Briefing for a Descent into Hell.* New York: Knopf, 1971, reprinted New York: Vintage, 1981.)

Index

Index